The
Art of
Divine
Contentment

by
Thomas Watson

Edited by Dr. Don Kistler

Soli Deo Gloria Publications
. . . *for instruction in righteousness* . . .

Soli Deo Gloria Publications
A division of Soli Deo Gloria Ministries, Inc.
P. O. Box 451, Morgan, PA 15064
(412) 221-1901/FAX 221-1902
www.SDGbooks.com

*

*

ISBN 1-57358-113-5

*

A workbook is available from
Marti Wibbels
610 West 28th Street
Kearney, NE 68845-4363
contentment@truthworks.us

Contents

Epistle to the Reader   v

To the Christian Reader   viii

Chapter 1   1
Introduction to the Text

Chapter 2   3
The First Branch of the Text

Chapter 3   7
The Second Proposition

Chapter 4   11
The Second Branch of the Text

Chapter 5   17
Resolving Some Questions

Chapter 6   19
The Nature of Contentment

Chapter 7   22
Reasons Pressing to Holy Contentment

Chapter 8　　　　　　　　　　　　　　　　26
The First Use: How a Christian May
Make This Life Comfortable

Chapter 9　　　　　　　　　　　　　　　　28
The Second Use: A Check to the
Discontented Christian

Chapter 10　　　　　　　　　　　　　　　31
The Third Use: A Persuasion to Contentment

Chapter 11　　　　　　　　　　　　　　　58
Divine Motives to Contentment

Chapter 12　　　　　　　　　　　　　　　99
Three Necessary Cautions

Chapter 13　　　　　　　　　　　　　　106
How a Christian May Know Whether
He Has Learned This Divine Art

Chapter 14　　　　　　　　　　　　　　112
Rules about Contentment

Chapter 15　　　　　　　　　　　　　　132
Use of Comfort

Epistle to the Reader

Christian Reader,

Having seriously considered the great dishonor done to almighty God (as well as the prejudice which accrues to ourselves) by the sin of discontent (a universal and epidemic sin), it put me upon the study of this subject at first. Nor is it incongruous to handle this next in order to "The Christian Charter" [reprinted by Soli Deo Gloria in *The Sermons of Thomas Watson*], I showed you there the great things which a believer has in reversion. Things to come are his, and here behold a Christian's holy and gracious deportment in this life, which reveals itself in nothing more eminently than in being content.

Discontent is to the soul as a disease is to the body: it puts it out of temper and much hinders its regular and sublime motions heavenward. Discontent is hereditary, and, no doubt, is much augmented by the many sad eclipses and changes that have fallen out of late in the political body, yet the disease is not to be excused because it is natural, but resisted because it is sinful. That which should put us out of love with this sullen distemper is the contemplation of the beautiful queen of contentment.

For my part, I do not know of any ornament in religion that more bespangles a Christian, or glitters in the eye of God and man more, than this of contentment. Nor certainly is there anything wherein all the Christian virtues work more harmoniously or shine more transparently than in this orb. Every grace acts its part here. This is the true philosopher's stone which turns all into gold. This is the curious enamel and embroidery of the heart which makes Christ's spouse all glorious within. How should every Christian be ambitious to wear such a sparkling diamond!

If there is a blessed life before we come to heaven, it is the contented life. And why not be contented? Why are you angry, and why is your countenance fallen? Man, of all creatures, has the least cause to be discontented. Can you deserve anything from God? Does He owe you anything? What if the scene were to turn and God put you under the blackrod? Whereas He now uses a rod, He might use a scorpion. He might as well damn you as whip you. Why, then, are you discontented? Why do you give way to this irrational and hurtful sin of discontent? May the good Lord humble His own people for nourishing such a viper in their breast as not only cuts out the bowels of their comfort, but spits venom in the face of God Himself!

Oh, Christian, if you are overspread with this fretting leprosy, you carry the man of sin about you, for you set yourself above God and act as if you were wiser than He, and would sassily prescribe to Him what condition is best for you! Oh, this devil of discontent which, whenever it possesses a person, makes his heart a little hell!

I know there will never be perfect contentment in this life. Perfect pleasure is only at God's right hand, yet we may begin here to tune our instrument before we play the sweet lesson of contentment exactly in heaven. I should be glad if this little piece might be like Moses' casting the tree into the waters, to make the bitter condition of life more sweet and pleasant to drink of.

I have once more ventured to address the public. I acknowledge this work to be homespun. Some better hand might have made a more effective draft, but, having preached upon the subject, I was earnestly solicited by some of my hearers to publish it, and although it is not dressed in that rich attire of eloquence as it might have been, I am not about poetry or oratory, but divinity. Nor is this intended for fancy, but practice.

If I may herein do any service, or cast but a mite into the treasury of the church's grace, I have my desire. The end of our living is to live to God, and to lift up His name in the world. May the Lord add an effectual blessing to this work and fasten it as a nail in a sure place. May He, of His mercy, make it as spiritual medicine to purge the ill humor of discontent out of our hearts, so that a crown of honor may be set upon the head of religion, and the crystal streams of joy and peace ever run in our souls. This is the prayer of him who is desirous to be a faithful orator for you at the throne of grace,

Thomas Watson

From my study at Stephens, Walbrook
May 5, 1653

To The Christian Reader

"A word spoken in due season, how good is it!" (Proverbs 15:23). As God "giveth to His creatures their meat in due season" (Psalm 104:27), so His "faithful stewards provide for His household their portion of meat in due season" (Luke 12:42). And as it is with corporal food—the season adds much, both to the value and usefulness thereof—in like manner it is with spiritual food. In this regard, the brokenness of these times (wherein the bosoms of most people are filled with alarm, and their mouths with murmurings) may well render this treatise all the more acceptable. The seas are not as stormy as men's spirits are tempestuous, tossed to and fro with discontents.

And now the Lord, who "maketh everything beautiful in His time" (Ecclesiastes 3:11), has most opportunely put into your hand a profitable discourse to calm unquiet hearts. Adam, in paradise, dashed upon the rock of discontent, which some divines conceive was his first sin. This, with many other instances in Scripture, together with our own sad experience, both identifies our danger and calls for caution. Now godliness is the only sovereign antidote against this spreading disease, and God's grace alone, being settled and exercised in the heart, can cause steadiness in stormy times. Whereas "contentment arises either from the fruition of all comforts, or from not desiring some which we have not," said Dr. [Joseph] Hall. True piety puts a Christian into such a position. Hereby we both possess God and are taught how to apply Him who is the only satisfying, everlasting portion of His people. Herein

Christ, though poor in this world, greatly rejoiced. "The Lord is the portion of my inheritance; the lines are fallen unto me in pleasant places, yea, I have a goodly heritage" (Psalm 16:5–2). Upon this account also Jacob said, "I have enough" (Genesis 33:11), or, as the original renders it, "I have all."

God the Father and Christ His Son had sweet satisfaction in each other when there was no other human being; therefore those who possess and improve God through Christ cannot possibly be dissatisfied. The Almighty is the God of all grace (1 Peter 5:10), all comfort (2 Corinthians 1:4), and of salvation (Psalm 68:20), in which respects neither deficiencies nor disappointments, losses nor crosses can cause disquieting discontents in that bosom where faith is commander-in-chief. The prophet Habakkuk rejoiced in the God of His salvation when the pestilence went before him and burning coals came forth of his feet (Habakkuk 3:5, 17–18), and when he supposed all creature succors both for delight and necessity to be quite removed. This is the life toward which Christians should endeavor, and which they may attain by the vigorous, regular actings of precious faith. This is the gain of contentment which comes in by godliness when providences are black and likely to be bloody.

"Now the just shall live by faith" (Habakkuk 2:4). That speech of learned Mr. [Thomas] Gataker is weighty and well worth marking: "A contented mind argues a religious heart, and a discontented mind argues an irreligious heart." And that worthy divine Mr. [Richard] Greenham was bold to say, "They never felt God's love, or tasted forgiveness of sin, who are discontented." This likewise was a holy breathing of Reverend Dr. [Joseph] Hall in his *Meditations*: "I have somewhat of the best things. I with thankfulness enjoy them, and will lack the rest with contentment." By attaining and maintaining this frame of heart, we might have much of heaven on this side of heaven. Holy contentment makes them truly rich whom the oppressing world makes very poor. Hereby our sweetest morsels shall be well seasoned, and our most bitter portions well sweetened.

Had we learned to enjoy contentment in Jehovah, who is immutable and all-sufficient, this heavenly frame of spirit would never perish or change in the midst of the most amazing alterations in church and state with which his Majesty is pleased to exercise us. Because we depend on outward things, therefore we are apt to die upon the nest through dejectedness, upon the approach of imagined dangers. When God sees cause to cut us short of many creature accommodations, faith will moderate our desires after them, assuring the soul that nothing is withdrawn or withheld which might really be advantageous; and doubtless it is a great piece of happiness upon earth not to long after that which the Lord is pleased to deny. Indeed, men act rather like heathens than Christians when they fret upon some particular inferior disappointments, notwithstanding God's liberality laid upon them in many other respects. Alexander, the Monarch of the world, was discontent because ivy would not grow in his gardens at Babylon. Diogenes the Cynic was herein more wise who, finding a mouse in his satchel, said that he saw that he was not so poor but that some were glad to have what he left behind.

Oh, how might we, if we had hearts to recognize higher providences, rock our peevish spirits quiet by much stronger arguments! Let us, then, lay before our eyes the practices of pious men recorded in Scripture for our imitation, such as Jacob (Genesis 28:20), Agur (Proverbs 30:8), and Paul (1 Timothy 6:8). And let us charge home upon our consciences divine exhortations backed with strong reasons and encouraged with sweet promises. It was the grave counsel of holy [Richard] Greenham, "Having food and raiment, take the rest as an overage."

Are we not less than the least of God's mercies? Is not God our bountiful Benefactor? Why, then, do we not rest contented with His liberal allowance? Oh, let us chide our wrangling spirits and encourage confidence with contentment in God as blessed David did!

My pen has outrun my purpose for this preface, so I will no longer detain you, good reader, wherein I have designed to quicken and to prepare you for the more fruitful use of this seasonable treatise, wherein the author has exercised to good purpose the Christian graces and the ministerial gifts with which God has enriched him.

Herein the doctrine of Christian contentment is clearly illustrated and profitably applied. The special cases wherein, through change of providences, discontents are most commonly occasioned are particularized, and are preservatives applied to the soul. Although some other worthy divines have been helpful to the Church of God by their discourses upon this subject, yet there is much of peculiar use in this treatise. The apostle tells us that some "manifestation of the Spirit is given unto everyone to profit withal" (1 Corinthians 12:7). Your soul's profit is propounded as the author's end in publishing this piece. That this end may be accomplished is the unfeigned desire and hearty prayer of him who is your servant in and for Christ,

Simeon Ashe

Chapter 1

Introduction to the Text

"I have learned, in whatsoever state I am,
therewith to be content." Philippians 4:11

These words are brought in by way of prolepsis to anticipate and prevent an objection. The apostle had, in the former verses, laid down many grave and heavenly exhortations, among them to "be careful for nothing" (verse 6). This is not to exclude a prudential care, for "he that provideth not for his own house has denied the faith, and is worse than an infidel" (1 Timothy 5:8); nor a religious care, for we must give all "diligence to make our calling and election sure" (2 Peter 1:10); but to exclude all anxious care about the issues and events of life: "Take no thought for your life, what you shall eat" (Matthew 6:25). And in this sense it should be a Christian's care not to be careful. The word "careful" in the Greek comes from a root that signifies to cut the heart in pieces, a soul-dividing care. Take heed of this. We are bid to "commit our way unto the Lord" (Psalm 37:5). The Hebrew word means to "roll thy way upon the Lord." It is our work to cast care, and it is God's work to take care. By our immoderacy we take His work out of His hands.

Care, when it is either distrustful or distracting, is very dishonorable to God. It takes away His providence, as if He sat in heaven and did not mind what became of things here below, like a man who makes a clock and then leaves

1

it to go by itself. Immoderate care takes the heart off from better things, and usually, while we are thinking how we shall live, we forget how to die. Care is a spiritual canker that wastes and discourages, and what good do we get from it? We may sooner add a furlong to our grief than a cubit of comfort by our care. God threatens it as a curse: "They shall eat their bread with carefulness" (Ezekiel 12:19). It is better to fast than to eat of that bread. "Be careful for nothing."

Now, lest anyone should say, "Yes, Paul, you preach that to us which you have scarcely learned yourself! Have you learned not to be careful?" the apostle seems tacitly to answer that objection in the words of the text: "I have learned, in whatsoever state I am, therewith to be content."

This is a speech worthy to be engraved upon our hearts, and to be written in letters of gold upon the crowns and diadems of princes. The text branches itself into these two general parts:

I. The scholar, Paul: "I have learned";
II. The lesson: "in every state to be content."

Chapter 2

The First Branch of the Text

I begin with the first, the scholar and his declaration, "I have learned," out of which I shall observe two things by way of paraphrase.

First, the apostle does not say, "I have heard that in every state I should be content," but, "I have learned."

DOCTRINE 1: It is not enough for Christians to hear their duty, but they must learn their duty. It is one thing to hear and another thing to learn, just as it is one thing to eat and another thing to cook. St. Paul was a practitioner. Christians hear much but, it is to be feared, learn little. There were four sorts of ground in the parable of Luke 8:5–8, and only one good ground—an emblem of this truth that there are many hearers, but few learners. There are two things that keep us from learning:

1. Slighting what we hear. Christ is the pearl of great price. When we disesteem this pearl, we shall never learn its value or its virtue. The gospel is a rare mystery: in one place it is called "the gospel of grace," in another "the gospel of glory," because in it, as in a transparent glass, the glory of God is resplendent. But he who has learned to condemn this mystery will hardly ever learn to obey it. He who looks upon the things of heaven as things by the by, and perhaps conducting a trade or carrying on some political design to be of greater importance—this man is on the high road to damnation and will hardly ever learn the things of his peace. Who will learn that which he thinks is

scarcely worth learning?

2. Forgetting what we hear. If a scholar has his rules laid before him and forgets them as fast as he reads them, he will never learn. Aristotle calls the memory "the scribe of the soul" and Bernard calls it "the stomach of the soul" because it has a retentive faculty and turns heavenly food into blood and spirit. We have great memories in other things. We remember that which is vain. Cyrus could remember the name of every soldier in his huge army. We remember injuries. This is to fill a precious cabinet with dung!

But how easily do we forget good! As Jerome said, "How soon we forget the sacred truths of God!" We are apt to forget three things: our faults, our friends, and our instructions. Many Christians are like sieves. Put a sieve into the water and it is full, but take it forth from the water and all runs out. So while they are hearing a sermon they remember something, but take the sieve out of the water—as soon as they have gone out of the church—and all is forgotten. "Let these sayings sink down into your ears," said Christ in Luke 9:44, or, as it is in the original, "Put these sayings into your ears." A man who would hide a jewel from being stolen locks it up safely in his chest. Let them sink down. The Word must not only fall as dew that wets the leaf, but as rain which soaks to the root of the tree and makes it fruitful. Oh, how often Satan, that fowl of the air, picks up the good seed that is set down!

Let this put you upon a serious trial. Some of you have heard much. You have lived forty, fifty, sixty years under the blessed trumpet of the gospel. What have you learned? You may have heard a thousand sermons and yet not learned one. Search your consciences. You have heard much against sin. Are you hearers or are you scholars?

How many sermons have you heard against covetousness, that it is the root on which pride, idolatry, and treason grow? One calls it a complex sin, which brings a great many sins with it. There is hardly any sin but covetousness is a main ingredient of it, and yet men are like the two daughters of the horseleech that cry, "Give, give." How much have you heard against rash anger, that it is a short frenzy, a dry drunkenness, that it rests in the bosom of fools (Ecclesiastes 7:9), and yet upon the least occasion your spirits begin to take fire?

How much have you heard against swearing? It is Christ's expressed mandate, "Swear not at all" (Matthew 5:34). This sin, of all others, may be termed "the unfruitful work of darkness" (Ephesians 5:11). It is neither sweetened with pleasure nor enriched with profit, the usual vermilion wherewith Satan paints sin. Swearing is forbidden with a curse. While the swearer shoots his oaths like flying arrows at God to pierce His glory, God shoots a flying roll of curses against him; and do you make your tongue a racket by which you toss oaths like tennis balls? Do you sport yourselves with oaths as did the Philistines with Samson, which will at last pull your house down around your ears? Alas! How have they learned what sin is who have not yet learned to leave sin? Does he know what a viper is who plays with it?

You have heard much of Christ; have you learned Christ? The Jews, as Jerome has said, carried Christ in their Bibles, but not in their hearts. Their sound went into all the earth (Romans 10:18). The prophets and apostles were as trumpets whose sound went abroad into the world, yet many thousands who heard the noise of these trumpets had not learned Christ: "They have not all obeyed" (verse 16).

A man may know much of Christ and yet not learn Christ. The devils knew Christ (Mark 1:34).

A man may preach Christ and yet not learn Christ, as did Judas and the pseudo-apostles (Philippians 1:15).

A man may profess Christ and yet not learn Christ. There are many professors in the world whom Christ will profess against (Matthew 7:22–23).

QUESTION. What is it, then, to learn Christ?

ANSWER 1. To learn Christ is to be made like Christ, when the divine characters of His holiness are engraved upon our hearts. "We all with open face, beholding as in a glass the glory of the Lord, are changed into the same image" (2 Corinthians 3:18). There is a metamorphosis: a sinner viewing Christ's image in the glass of the gospel is transformed into that image. Never did any man look upon Christ with a spiritual eye but went away quite changed. A true saint is a divine landscape or picture where all the rare beauties of Christ are portrayed in a lively manner and drawn forth. He has the same Spirit, the same judgment, and the same will with Jesus Christ.

ANSWER 2. To learn Christ is to believe in Him as "my Lord and my God" (John 20:28). It is when we not only believe God, but believe *in* God, which is the actual application of Christ to ourselves, and is, as it were, the spreading of the sacred medicine of His blood upon our souls. You who have heard much of Christ, and yet cannot with a humble adherence say, "my Jesus," be not offended if I tell you that the devil can say his creed as well as you.

ANSWER 3. To learn Christ is to live Christ. When we have Bible conduct, our lives, like rich diamonds, cast a sparkling luster in the church of God (Philippians 1:27), and are, in some sense, parallel with the life of Christ, as the transcript is to the original.

1 made like him
2 believe in him
3 live christ

Chapter 3

The Second Proposition

These words "I have learned" are words that import difficulty; they show how difficultly the apostle came by his contentment of mind. It was not a natural thing. St. Paul did not come by it naturally, but he had learned it. It cost him many prayers and tears; it was taught to him by the Spirit. From this comes:

DOCTRINE 2: Good things are hard to come by. The business of religion is not as easy as most imagine. "I have learned," said Paul. Indeed, you need not teach a man to sin; this is natural, and therefore facile. It comes as water out of a spring. It is an easy thing to be wicked. Hell will be taken without a storm; but the matter of religion must be learned. To cut the flesh is easy, but to prick a vein and not cut an artery is hard.

The trade of sin does not need to be learned, but the art of divine contentment is not achieved without holy industry. "I have learned."

There are two pregnant reasons why there must be so much study and exercise:

1. Because spiritual things are against nature. Everything in religion is contrary to nature. There are in religion two things, *credenda* and *facienda*, and both are against nature. *Credenda* deals with matters of faith. For a man to be justified by the righteousness of another, to become a fool that he may be wise, to save all by losing all—this is against nature. *Facienda* deals with matters of prac-

tice. The first of these is self-denial. For a man to deny his own wisdom and see himself as blind; to deny his own will and have it melted into the will of God; to pluck out the right eye, beheading and crucifying that sin which is the favorite and lies nearest to the heart; to be dead to the world, and in the midst of want to abound; to take up the cross and follow Christ, not only in golden, but bloody paths; to embrace religion when it is dressed in its night clothes, all the jewels of honor and preferment being pulled off,—this is against nature, and therefore must be learned.

Another of these matters is self-examination. For a man to take his heart (like a watch) all in pieces; to set up a spiritual inquisition or court of conscience and traverse things in his own soul; to take David's candle and lantern (Psalm 119:105) and search for sin, nay, as judge to pass the sentence upon himself—this is against nature, and will not easily be attained without learning.

Another is self-reformation. To see a man like Caleb, of another spirit, walking contrary to himself, the current of his life altered and running into the channel of religion—this is wholly against nature. When a stone ascends, it is not a natural motion, but a violent motion. The motion of the soul heavenward is a violent motion; it must therefore be learned. Flesh and blood is not skilled in these things. Nature can no more cast out nature than Satan can cast out Satan.

2. Because spiritual things are above nature. There are some things in nature that are hard to find out, such as the causes of things, which are not learned without study. Aristotle, a great philosopher (whom some have called an eagle fallen from the clouds), yet could not find out the motion of the river Euripus, and therefore threw himself

into it. What, then, are divine things, which are in a sphere above nature and beyond all human distinction, such as the Trinity, the hypostatic union, or the mystery of faith to believe against hope? Only God's Spirit can light our candle here. The apostle calls these "the deep things of God" (1 Corinthians 2:10). The gospel is full of jewels, but they are locked up from sense and reason. The angels in heaven are searching into these sacred depths (1 Peter 1:12).

USE. Let us beg the Spirit of God to teach us, for we must be divinely taught. The eunuch could read, but he could not understand until Philip joined himself to his chariot (Acts 8:29). God's Spirit must join Himself to our chariot. He must teach or we cannot learn. "All thy children shall be taught of the Lord" (Isaiah 54:13). A man may read the figure on the sundial, but he cannot tell how the day goes unless the sun shines on the dial. We may read the Bible over, but we cannot learn its purpose until the Spirit of God "shines into our hearts" (2 Corinthians 4:6).

Oh, implore this blessed Spirit; it is God's royal prerogative to teach. "I am the Lord thy God, that teacheth thee to profit" (Isaiah 48:17). Ministers may tell us our lesson, but only God can teach us. We have lost both our hearing and our eyesight; therefore we are very unfit to learn. Ever since Eve listened to the serpent, we have been deaf; and since she looked on the tree of knowledge, we have been blind. But when God comes to teach, He removes these impediments. We are naturally dead, and who will go about to teach a dead man? Yet, behold! God undertakes to make dead men understand mysteries! God is the grand Teacher.

This is the reason why the Word preached works so

differently upon men. Two are in a pew. One is wrought upon effectually, yet the other lies at the ordinances as a dead child at the breast and gets no nourishment. What is the reason? Because the heavenly gale of the Spirit blows upon one and not upon the other. One has the anointing of God which teaches him all things (1 John 2:27); the other has it not. God's Spirit speaks sweetly, but irresistibly. In that heavenly doxology none could sing the new song but those who were "sealed in their foreheads" (Revelation 14:1). Reprobates could not sing it. Those who are skillful in the mysteries of salvation must have the seal of the Spirit upon them.

Let us make this our prayer: "Lord, breathe Thy Spirit into Thy Word." And we have a promise which may add wings to our prayer: "If ye, then, being evil, know how to give good gifts to your children, how much more shall your heavenly Father give His Spirit to them that ask Him?" (Luke 11:13).

And so much for the first part of the text on Paul the scholar.

Chapter 4

The Second Branch of the Text

I come now to the second branch, which is the main thing, the lesson itself: "In whatsoever state I am, therewith to be content."

Here was a rare piece of learning, indeed, and certainly more to be wondered at in Paul (that he knew how to turn himself to every condition) than all the learning in the world besides, which has been so applauded in former ages by Julius Caesar, Ptolemy, Xenophon, and all the great admirers of learning.

The text has only a few words in it, "in every state content," but if that is true which Fulgentius once said, that the most golden sentence is ever measured by brevity and suavity, then this is a most accomplished speech. The text is like a precious jewel: little in quantity, but great in worth and value.

The main proposition I shall insist upon is this: a gracious spirit is a contented spirit. The doctrine of contentment is very superlative, and until we have learned this we have not learned to be Christians.

1. It is a hard lesson. The angels in heaven had not learned it; they were not content. Though their state was glorious, yet they were still soaring aloft and aimed at something higher. Jude 6: "The angels which kept not their first estate." They kept not their state because they were not content with their state. Our first parents, clothed with the white robe of innocence in paradise,

11

had not learned to be content. They had aspiring hearts and, thinking their human nature too low and homespun, wanted to be crowned with deity and be as gods (Genesis 3:5). Though they had the choice of all the trees in the garden, yet none would satisfy them but the tree of knowledge, which they supposed would have been as eye-salve to make them omniscient. Oh, then, if this lesson was so hard to learn in innocence, how hard shall we find it who are clogged with corruption?

2. It is of universal extent, and concerns all. It concerns rich men. One would think it needless to press those to contentment whom God has blessed with great estates, but rather persuade them to be humble and thankful. No, I am saying, be content. Rich men have their discontents as well as others, as appears when they have a great estate, yet are discontented that they have no more. They would make the hundred talents a thousand. The more wine a man drinks, the more he thirsts. Covetousness is a dry dropsy. An earthly heart is like the grave: it is never satisfied. Therefore, I say to you rich men, be content.

If we may suppose rich men to be content with their estates (which is very seldom), yet, though they have enough estate, they do not have enough honor. If their barns are full enough, yet their turrets are not high enough. They would be somebody in the world, as "Theudas, who boasted himself to be somebody" (Acts 5:36). They never go so cheerfully as when the wind of honor and applause fills their sails. If this wind is down, they are discontented. One would think Haman had as much as his proud heart could desire. He was set above all the princes, advanced upon the pinnacle of honor to be the second man in the kingdom, yet in the

midst of all his pomp, because Mordecai would not un-
cover and kneel, he was discontented and full of wrath
(Esther 3:1–5). And there was no way to assuage this
pleurisy of revenge but by shedding all the Jews' blood
and offering them up in sacrifice. The itch of honor is
seldom allayed without blood; therefore, I say to you
rich men, be content.

Rich men, if we may suppose them to be content
with their honor and magnificent titles, yet do not always have contentment in their relations. She who lies
in the bosom may sometimes blow the coals, as Job's
wife, who in a fit would have him fall out with God
Himself: "Curse God and die."

Sometimes children cause discontent. How often is
it seen that the mother's milk nourishes a viper, that
he who once sucked her breast goes about to suck her
blood? Parents often, of grapes, gather thorns, and of
figs thistles. Children are sweet briars, like the rose
which is a fragrant flower, but, as Basil said, has its
prickles. Our relative comforts are not all pure wine,
but mixed. They have in them more dregs than spirits,
and are like that river Plutarch speaks of where the waters run sweet in the morning, but bitter in the
evening. We have no exemption granted to us in this
life. Therefore, rich men need to be called upon to be
content.

The doctrine of contentment also concerns poor
men. You who suck so liberally from the doctrine of
providence, be content. It is a hard lesson; therefore it
needs to be set upon all the sooner. How hard is it,
when the livelihood is gone, when a great estate is
boiled away almost to nothing, then to be content? The
means of subsistence is called in Scripture "our life"

because it is the very sinews of life. The woman in Luke
8:43 spent all her living upon the physicians. In the
Greek it says that she spent her whole life on the physicians, because she spent her means by which she
should live. It is much, when poverty has clipped our
wings, then to be content; but though it is hard it is excellent, and the apostle here had learned in every state
to be content.

God had brought Paul into as great a variety of conditions as ever we read of any man, and yet he was content. Otherwise he could never have gone through it
with so much cheerfulness. See into what vicissitudes
this blessed apostle was cast. "We are troubled on every
side" (2 Corinthians 4:8)—there was the sadness of his
condition; "but not distressed"—there was his contentment in that condition. We are perplexed"—there is his
affliction; "but not in despair"—there is his contentment. And if we read a little further he says, "in afflictions, in necessities, in distresses, in stripes, in impris-
onments, in tumults" and so on; there is his trouble,
and behold his contentment, "as having nothing, yet
possessing all things" (2 Corinthians 6:4–10). When the
apostle was driven out of all, yet with regard to that
sweet contentment of mind (which was like music in
his soul), he possessed all. We read a short map or his-
tory of his sufferings: "in prisons more frequent, in
deaths oft" (2 Corinthians 11:23). Yet behold the
blessed frame and temper of his spirit: "I have learned,
in whatsoever state I am, therewith to be content."

Whichever way Providence blew, he had such heavenly skill and dexterity that he knew how to steer his
course. As for his outward state, he was indifferent. He
could either be on the top of Jacob's ladder or on the

bottom. He could sing a dirge or an anthem. He could be anything that God would have him be: "I know how to want, and how to abound." Here is a rare pattern for us to imitate.

In regard to his faith and courage, Paul was like a cedar: he could not be stirred. But as for his outward condition, he was like a reed, bending every way with the wind of Providence. When a prosperous gale blew upon him, he could bend with that ("I know how to be full"), and when a boisterous gust of affliction blew, he could bend in humility with that ("I know how to be hungry"). Paul was, as Aristotle says, like a die that has four squares. Throw it whichever way you will, it still falls upon its bottom. Let God throw the apostle whichever way He would, he fell upon this foundation of contentment.

A contented spirit is like a watch. Though you carry it up and down with you, yet the spring of it is not shaken, nor the wheels out of order. The watch keeps its perfect motion. So it was with Paul. Though God had carried him into various conditions, he was not lifted up with one, nor cast down with the other. The spring of his heart was not broken; the wheels of his affections were not disordered, but kept their constant motion towards heaven. The ship that lies at anchor may sometimes be a little shaken, but never sinks. Flesh and blood may have its fears and disquiets, but grace checks them. Having cast anchor in heaven, a Christian's heart never sinks. A gracious spirit is a contented spirit.

This is a rare art. Paul did not learn it at the feet of Gamaliel. "I am instructed," he said (verse 12). "I am initiated into this holy mystery." It is as if he had said, "I have gotten the divine art. I have the knack of it." God must make us right artists. If we should put some men to an art that they are not skilled in, how unfit would they be for it! Put a husbandman to painting or drawing pictures, and what strange work would he make! This is out of his sphere. Take a painter who is exact in laying colors and put him to plowing, or set him to planting and growing trees; this is not his art, and he is not skilled in it. If you bid a natural man to live by faith, and to be content when all things go contrary, you bid him to do that which he has no skill in; you may as well bid a child to guide the stern of a ship.

To live contented upon God in the deficiency of comforts is an art which "flesh and blood hath not revealed." Nay, many of God's children who excel in some duties of religion, when they come to this one of contentment, how they bungle! They have hardly begun to be masters of this art.

Chapter 5

Resolving Some Questions

QUESTION 1. May not a Christian be sensible of his condition and yet be content?

ANSWER. Yes, otherwise he is not a saint, but a stoic. Rachel did well to weep for her children (there was nature), but her fault was that she refused to be comforted (there was discontent). Christ Himself was sensible when He sweated great drops of blood and said, "Father, if it be possible, let this cup pass from Me" (Matthew 26:39), yet He was content and sweetly submitted His will: "Nevertheless, not as I will, but as Thou wilt." The apostle bids us to "humble ourselves under the mighty hand of God" (1 Peter 5:6), which we cannot do unless we are sensible of it.

QUESTION 2. May a Christian lay open his grievances to God and still be content?

ANSWER. Yes. "Unto Thee have I opened my cause" (Jeremiah 20:12). David poured out his complaint before the Lord (Psalm 142:2). We may cry to God and desire Him to write down all our injuries. Shall not the child complain to the Father? When any burden is upon the spirit, prayer gives vent; it eases the heart. Hannah's spirit was burdened. She said, "I am a woman of a troubled spirit" (1 Samuel 1:15). Having prayed and wept, she went away and was sad no more. Here is the difference between a holy complaint and a discontented complaint. In the one we complain *to* God; in the other we complain *of* God.

17

QUESTION 3. What is it that contentment excludes?

ANSWER. There are three things which contentment banishes out of its diocese, and which can by no means consist with it.

_1. It excludes a vexatious repining; this is properly the daughter of discontent. "I mourn in my complaint" (Psalm 55:2). He does not say, "I murmur in my complaint." Murmuring is no better than mutiny in the heart; it is a rising up against God. When the sea is rough and unquiet, it casts forth nothing but foam. When the heart is discontented, it casts forth the foam of anger, impatience, and sometimes little better than blasphemy. Murmuring is nothing else but the scum which boils off from a discontented heart.

_2. It excludes an uneven discomposure, as when a man says, "I am in such straits that I do not know how to move or get out. I shall be undone." Head and heart are so taken up that a man is not fit to pray or meditate; he is not himself. When an army is routed, one man runs this way and another that way, and the army is put into disorder. So a discontented man's thoughts run up and down distracted. Discontent dislocates and disjoints the soul; it pulls off the wheels.

_3. It excludes a childish despondency, which is usually a result of the discomposure just discussed. A man, being in a hurry of mind, not knowing which way to extricate or wind himself out of the present trouble, begins to faint and sink under it. For care is to the mind as a burden is to the back: it loads the spirits and, with overloading, sinks them. A despondent spirit is a discontented spirit.

Chapter 6

The Nature of Contentment

Having answered these questions, I shall, in the next place, come to describe this contentment. It is a sweet temper of spirit whereby a Christian carries himself in an equal poise in every condition. The nature of this will appear more clearly in three aphorisms.

1. Contentment is a divine thing; it becomes ours, not by acquisition, but by infusion. It is a slip taken off from the tree of life and planted by the Spirit of God in the soul. It is a fruit that grows not in the garden of philosophy, but is of a heavenly birth. It is, therefore, very observable that contentment is joined with godliness. "But godliness with contentment is great gain" (1 Timothy 6:6).

Contentment being a consequence of godliness, or concomitant, or both, I call it divine to distinguish it from that contentment at which a moral man may arrive. Heathens seem to have this contentment, but it is only the shadow and picture of it—the beryll, not the true diamond. Theirs is but civil; this is sacred. Theirs is only from principles of reason; this is of religion. Theirs is lit only at nature's torch, this one at the lamp of Scripture. Reason may teach contentment a little, as thus: "Whatever my condition is, this is that to which I am born. If I meet with crosses, it is but a universal misery. All have their share; why, therefore, should I be troubled?" Reason may suggest this and, indeed, this may be constraint rather than contentment; but to live securely and cheerfully upon God in

19

the abatement of creature supplies, religion alone can bring this into the soul's treasury.

2. Contentment is an intrinsic thing. It lies within a man not in the bark, but in the root. Contentment has both its fountain and stream in the soul. The beam does not have its light from the air. The beams of comfort which a contented man has do not arise extrinsically from foreign comforts, but from within. As sorrow is seated in the spirit ("the heart knows its own grief," Proverbs 14:10), so contentment lies within the soul and does not depend on externals. Hence I gather that outward troubles cannot hinder this blessed contentment. It is a spiritual thing and arises from spiritual grounds, namely the apprehension of God's love. When there is a tempest without, there may be music within. A bee may sting through the skin, but it cannot sting to the heart. Outward afflictions cannot sting to a Christian's heart where contentment lies. Thieves may plunder us of our money and silver, but not of this pearl of contentment, unless we are willing to part with it; for it is locked up in the cabinet of the heart. The soul which is possessed of this rich treasure of contentment is like Noah in the ark, who can sing in the midst of a deluge.

3. Contentment is a habitual thing; it shines with a fixed light in the firmament of the soul. Contentment does not appear only now and then, as some stars which are seldom seen. It is a settled temper of the heart. One action does not distinguish the character. He is not said to be a liberal man who gives alms once in his life (a covetous man may do so); but he is said to be liberal who is "given to liberality" (Romans 12:13), that is, who upon all occasions is willing to indulge the necessities of the poor. So he is said to be a contented man who is given to con-

tentment. It is not casual, but constant. Aristotle, in his *Rhetoric*, distinguishes between colors in the face that arise from passion and those that arise from complexion. The pale face may look red when it blushed, but this is only a passion. He is said properly to be ruddy and sanguine who is constantly so; it is his complexion. He is not a contented man who is so occasionally, and perhaps when he is pleased, but who is so constantly. It is the habit and complexion of his soul.

Chapter 7

Reasons Pressing to Holy Contentment

Having opened the nature of contentment, I come next to lay down some reasons or arguments to contentment which may hold weight with us.

1. The first is God's precept. It is charged upon us as a duty: "Be content with such things as you have" (Hebrews 13:5). The same God who has bidden us believe has bidden us to be content. If we do not obey, we run ourselves into a spiritual warrant. God's Word is a sufficient warrant; it has authority in it and must be a sacred spell to remove discontent. "Ipse dixit" was enough among Pythagoras's scholars. "Be it enacted" is the royal style. God's Word must be the star that guides, and His will the weight that moves our obedience. His fiat is a law and has majesty enough in it to captivate us into obedience. Our hearts must not be more unquiet than the raging sea, which at His word is stilled (Matthew 8:26).

2. The second reason for contentment is God's promise, for He has said, "I will never leave thee, nor forsake thee" (Hebrews 13:5). God has engaged Himself under hand and seal for our necessary provisions. If a king should say to one of his subjects, "I will take care of you. As long as I have any crown revenues, you shall be provided for. If you are in danger, I will secure you; if in want, I will supply you," would not that subject be content? Behold, God has here made a promise to the believer and has, as it were, entered into bond for his security. "I will

22

never leave you." Shall not this charm down the devil of discontent? "Leave thy fatherless children with me, I will preserve them alive" (Jeremiah 49:11).

I think I see the godly man on his deathbed greatly discontented, and I hear him complaining, "What will become of my wife and children when I am dead and gone? They may come to poverty."

God says, "Do not trouble yourself; be content. I will take care of your children, and let your widow trust in Me." God has made a promise to us that He will not leave us, and has entailed the promise upon our wife and children; and will this not satisfy? True faith will take God's single bond without calling for witnesses.

3. Be content by virtue of a decree. Whatever our condition is, God, the great Umpire of the world, has decreed that condition for us, and by His providence has ordered all the things that go along with it. Let a Christian often think to himself, "Who has placed me here, whether I am in a higher sphere or in a lower? Not chance or fortune, as the totally blind heathens imagined; no, it is the wise God who has, by His providence, fixed me in this orb." We must act that scene which God will have us act. Do not say that such a one has occasioned this to you. Do not look too much at the underside of the wheel. We read in Ezekiel 1:16 of a wheel within a wheel. God's decree is the cause of the turning of the wheels, and His Providence is the inner wheel that moves all the rest. God's Providence is that helm which turns about the whole ship of the universe. Say, then, like holy David, "I was silent, because Thou, Lord, didst it" (Psalm 39:9). God's Providence, which is nothing but the carrying out of His decrees, should be a counterpoison against discontent. God has set us in our station, and has done it in wisdom.

We fancy such a condition of life good for us, whereas, if we were our own carvers, we should often cut the worst piece. Lot, being put to his choice, chose Sodom, which was soon after burned with fire. Rachel was very desirous of children: "Give me children or I die" (Genesis 30:1), and it cost her her life in bringing forth a child. Abraham was earnest for Ishmael: "Oh, that Ishmael may live before Thee!" (Genesis 17:18); but he had little comfort either of him or of his seed. He was born a son of strife; his hand was against every man, and every man's hand was against him. The disciples wept for Christ's leaving the world. They chose His corporal presence, whereas it was best for them that Christ should be gone, or else the Comforter would not come. David chose the life of his child. He wept and fasted for it, whereas, if the child had lived, it would have been a perpetual monument of his shame. We often stand in our own light; if we would sort or parcel out our own comforts, we would hit upon what is wrong. Is it not well for the child that the parent choose for it? Were it left alone, it would perhaps choose a knife to cut its own fingers. A man in a convulsion calls for wine which, if he had it, would be little better than poison. It is well for the patient that he is at the physician's appointment.

The consideration that there is a decree determining, and a Providence disposing, all things that fall out would work our hearts to holy contentment. The wise God has ordered our condition. If He sees that it is better for us to abound, we shall abound. And if He sees that it is better for us to want, we shall want. Be content to be at God's disposal.

God sees in His infinite wisdom that the same condition is not convenient for all. That which is good for one may be bad for another. One season of weather will not serve all men's occasions. One needs sunshine, another rain. One condition of life will not fit every man any more than one suit of clothing will fit every body. Prosperity is not fit for all, nor is adversity. If one man is brought low, perhaps he can bear it better. He has a greater stock of grace, more faith and patience. He can gather grapes of thorns, or pick some comfort out of the cross. Everyone cannot do this.

Another man is seated in an eminent place of dignity. He is more fit for it. Perhaps it is a place that requires more skill and judgment, of which everyone is not capable. Perhaps he can use his position better. He has a public heart as well as a public place. The wise God sees that condition to be bad for one which is good for another. Hence it is that He places men in different orbs and spheres—some higher, some lower. One man desires health, but God sees sickness to be better for him. God will work health out of sickness by bringing the body of death into a consumption. Another man desires liberty, but God sees restraint to be better for him. He will work out his liberty by restraint. When his feet are bound, his heart shall be most enlarged. If we believed this, it would give check to the sinful disputes and cavils of our hearts. Shall I be discontented at that which is enacted by a decree and ordered by Providence? Is this to be a child or a rebel?

Chapter 8

The First Use:
How a Christian May Make His Life Comfortable

Christian contentment shows us how a Christian may come to lead a comfortable life, even a heaven upon earth, be the times what they will. The comfort of life does not consist in having much. It is Christ's maxim: "Man's life consisteth not in the abundance of things which he doth possess" (Luke 12:15), but in being contented. Is not the bee as well contented with feeding on the dew or sucking from a flower as the ox that grazes on the mountains? Contentment lies within a man, in the heart, and the way to be comfortable is not by having our barns filled, but our mind quiet. "The contented man," said Seneca, "is the happy man." Discontent is a fretting humor which dries the brain, wastes the spirits, and corrodes and eats out the comfort of life. Discontent makes a man so that he does not enjoy what he possesses. A drop or two of vinegar will sour a whole glass of wine. Let a man have the affluence and confluence of worldly comforts, yet a drop or two of discontent will embitter and poison all. Comfort depends upon contentment. Jacob went halting when the sinew upon the hollow of his thigh shrank. In the same way, when the sinew of contentment begins to shrink, we go halting in our comforts.

Contentment is as necessary to keep the life comfortable as oil is necessary to keep the lamp burning. The clouds of discontent often drop the showers of tears. Would we have comfort in our lives? We may have it if we will. A Christian may carve out what condition he will for himself. Why do you complain of your troubles? It is not trouble that troubles, but discontent. It is not the water outside the ship, but the water that gets within the leak which drowns it. It is not outward affliction that can make the life of a Christian sad; a contented mind would sail above these waters. But when there is a leak of discontent open and trouble gets into the heart, then it is disquieted and sinks. Do, therefore, as the mariners: pump the water out and stop this spiritual leak in your soul, and no trouble can hurt you.

Chapter 9

The Second Use: A Check to the Discontented Christian

Here is a just reproof to those who are discontented with their condition. This disease is almost epidemic. Some who are not content with the callings into which God has set them must seek to go a step higher, from the plow to the throne; they, like the spider in Proverbs, will take hold with their hands and be in kings' palaces (Proverbs 30:28). Others would go from the shop to the pulpit. They would be in the temple of honor before they are in the temple of virtue; they step into Moses' chair without Aaron's bells and pomegranates. They are like apes who most show their deformity when they are climbing. It is not enough that God has bestowed gifts upon men in private to edify, that He has enriched them with many mercies, but they seek the priesthood also. What is this but discontent arising from high-flown pride? These people secretly tax the wisdom of God, that He has not raised them up in their condition a peg higher. Every man is complaining that his state is no better, though he seldom complains that his heart is no better! One man commends this kind of life, another commends that. One man thinks a country life is best, another a city life, as the poet Horatio elegantly expressed it:

> "O fortunate merchants," said the soldier, heavy with years and already weakened in his limbs with much labor.

28

> Against this the merchant, with the south winds buffeting his ship, said, "The military is better; for what reason? It fights in battle—a quick death comes in a very short time, or a happy victory."

The soldier thinks it best to be a merchant, and the merchant to be a soldier. Men can be content to be anything but what God would have them be. We may cry out with the same poet:

> Who makes it so, Maecenas, that no one to whom either his plan has given a lot in life, or to whom a fate has befallen, lives contented in that lot? Should a man praise those who follow opposite choices?

How is it that no man is content? Very few Christians have learned Paul's lesson. Neither poor nor rich know how to be content. They can learn anything but this.

If men are poor, they learn to be envious. They malign those who are above them. Another's prosperity is an eyesore. When God's candles shine upon their neighbor's tabernacle, this light offends them. In the midst of wants, men can, in this sense, abound—that is, in envy and malice. An envious eye is an evil eye. They learn to be querulous, still complaining as if God had dealt harshly with them. They are ever telling of their wants. They want this and that comfort, whereas their greatest want is a contented spirit. Those who are well enough content with their sins yet are not content with their condition.

If men are rich, they learn to be covetous, thirsting insatiably after the world, and by any unjust means scraping it together. "Their right hand is full of bribes," as the Psalmist expresses it (Psalm 26:10). Put a good cause in one scale and a piece of gold in the other, and the gold

weighs more. Solomon said that there are four things that
say, "It is not enough" (Proverbs 30:15). I may add a fifth,
the heart of a covetous man. Neither rich nor poor know
how to be content.

Certainly never since the creation did this sin of discontent reign, or rather rage, more than in our times.
Never was God more dishonored. You can hardly speak
with anyone but the passion of his tongue betrays the discontent of his heart. Everyone lisps out his trouble, and
here even the stammering tongue speaks too freely and
fluently. If we do not have what we desire, God shall not
have a good look from us; but presently we are sick from
discontent and ready to die out of a bad mood. If God will
not give the people of Israel what they desire, they bid
Him take their lives. They must have quails instead of
manna. Ahab, though a king (and one would think his
crown lands would have been sufficient for him), yet was
sullen and discontent for want of Naboth's vineyards.
Jonah, though a good man and a prophet, yet was ready to
die in a fit of sulking. And because God killed his gourd
he said, "Kill me, too!" Rachel said, "Give me children or I
die." She had many blessings if she could have seen them,
but lacked this contentment. God will supply our wants,
but must He satisfy our lusts, too?

Many are discontented over trifles. Someone has a
better dress, a richer jewel, or a newer fashion. Nero, not
content with his empire, was troubled that the musicians
had more skill in playing than he. How fantastic are some
who pine away in discontent for the want of those things
which, if they had them, would but render them more
ridiculous!

Chapter 10

The Third Use: A Persuasion to Contentment

Let this exhort us to labor for contentment. This is that which beautifies and bespangles a Christian, and, as spiritual embroidery, sets him off in the eyes of the world.

OBJECTION. But I think I hear some bitterly complaining and saying, "Alas, how is it possible to be contented? The Lord 'hath made my chain heavy' (Lamentations 3:7). He has cast me into a very sad condition."

ANSWER. There is no sin that does not labor either to hide itself under some mask or, if it cannot be concealed, then to vindicate itself by some apology. This sin of discontent I find very witty in its apologies, which I shall first reveal and then make a reply. We must lay it down as a rule that discontent is a sin, so that all the pretenses and apologies wherewith it labors to justify itself are only the paintings and dressings of a strumpet.

APOLOGY 1. "I have lost a child." Paulina, upon the loss of her children, was so possessed with a spirit of sadness that she would have entombed herself in her own discontent. Our love for relations is oftentimes more than our love for religion.

ANSWER 1. We must be content not only when God gives mercies, but when He takes them away. If we must "in everything give thanks" (1 Thessalonians 5:18), then we must in nothing be discontented.

ANSWER 2. Perhaps God has taken away the cistern that He may give you more of the spring. He has dark-

ened the starlight that you may have more of the sunlight.
God intends that you shall have more of Himself, and is
He not better than ten sons? Look not so much upon a
temporal loss as a spiritual gain. The comforts of the
world are dregs. Those which come out of the granary of
the promise are purer and sweeter.

ANSWER 3. Your child was not given, but lent. "I have
lent my son to the Lord," said Hannah (1 Samuel 1:28).
She lent him? The Lord had but lent him to her! Mercies
are not entailed upon us, but lent. What a man lends he
may call for again when he pleases. God has put out a
child to you for awhile to nurse; will you be displeased if
He takes His child home again? Oh, do not be discontented that a mercy is taken away from you, but rather be
thankful that it was lent to you for so long!

ANSWER 4. Suppose your child is taken from you.
Either he was good or bad. If he was rebellious, you have
not so much parted with a child as with a burden. You
grieve for that which might have been a greater grief to
you. If he was religious, then remember that he is taken
from the evil to come and placed in his center of felicity.
This lower region is full of gross and hurtful vapors. How
happy are those who are mounted into the celestial orbs!
"The righteous is taken away" (Isaiah 57:1). In the original
it is "he is gathered." A wicked child who dies is cut off,
but the pious child is gathered. Even as we see men gather
flowers and candy, and so preserve them, so God has
gathered your child as a sweet flower that He may cover it
with glory, and preserve it by Him forever. Why, then,
should a Christian be discontented? Why should he weep
excessively? "Daughters of Jerusalem, weep not for Me,
but weep for yourselves" (Luke 23:28).

Could we hear our children speaking to us out of

heaven, they would say, "Weep not for us who are happy; we lie upon a soft pillow, even in the bosom of Christ. The Prince of Peace is embracing us and kissing us with the kisses of His lips. Be not troubled at our preferment. Weep not for us, but weep for yourselves who are in a sinful world. You are in the valley of tears, but we are on the mountain of spices. We have gotten to our harbor, but you are still tossing on the waves of inconstancy." O Christian, do not be discontent that you have parted with such a child, but rather rejoice that you had such a child to part with. Break forth into thankfulness. What an honor is it to a parent to beget such a child, who while he lives increases the joy of the glorified angels, and when he dies increases the number of glorified saints!

ANSWER 5. If God has taken away one of your children, He has left you more. He could have stripped you of all. He took away all Job's comforts, his estates and his children; his wife was left, but as a cross. Satan made a bow of this rib (as Chrysostom says) and shot a temptation by her at Job, thinking to have shot him to the heart: "Curse God and die." But Job had upon him the breastplate of integrity. Though his children were taken away, yet not his graces. Still he was content, still he blessed God. Oh, think how many mercies you still enjoy! Yet our base hearts are more discontented at one loss than thankful for a hundred mercies. God has plucked one branch of grapes from you, but how many precious clusters are left behind?

"But it was my only child, the staff of my age, the seed of my comfort, and the only blossom out of which the honor of an ancient family grew!"

God has promised you, if you belong to Him, a name "better than of sons and daughters" (Isaiah 56:5). Is he dead who should have been the monument to have kept up the name of a family? God has given you a new name. He has written your name in the Book of Life. Behold your spiritual heraldry. Here is a name that cannot be cut off.

Has God taken away your only child? He has given His only Son. This is a happy exchange. What need does he have to complain of losses who has Christ? He is His Father's brightness (Hebrews 1:3), His fullness (Colossians 2:9), and His delight (Proverbs 8:30). Is there enough in Christ to delight the heart of God? And is there not enough in Him to ravish us with holy delight? He is wisdom to teach us, righteousness to acquit us, sanctification to adorn us. He is that royal and princely gift. He is the bread of angels (according to Bernard), the joy and triumph of saints. He is "all in all" (Colossians 3:11). Why, then, are you discontented? Though your child is lost, yet you have Him for whom all things are loss.

ANSWER 6. Let us blush to think that nature should seem to outstrip grace. When Pulvillus, a heathen, was about to consecrate a temple to Jupiter, and news was brought to him of the death of his son, he would not desist from his enterprise, but with much composure of mind gave orders for his decent burial.

APOLOGY 2. "I have a great part of my estate strangely melted away, and trading is beginning to fail."

ANSWER. God is sometimes pleased to bring His children very low and cut them short in their estate. It fares with them as with the widow who had nothing in her house except a pot of oil (2 Kings 4:2); but be content.

1. God has taken away your estate, but not your portion. This is a sacred paradox. Honor and estate are no part of a Christian's jointure; they are accessories rather

than essentials. They are extrinsic and foreign; therefore the loss of these cannot designate a man as being miserable. Still the portion remains: " 'The Lord is my portion,' saith my soul" (Lamentations 3:24). Suppose one were worth millions, and he should lose a pin off his sleeve. This is no part of his estate, nor would we say that he is undone. The loss of earthly comforts is not so much to a Christian's portion as the loss of a pin is to a million. "These things shall be added to you" (Matthew 6:33). They shall be cast in as a surplus.

When a man buys a piece of cloth, he has an inch or two extra given beyond the measure. Now, though he loses his inch of cloth, yet he is not undone, for still the whole piece remains. Our outward estate is even less in comparison to our true the portion as an inch of cloth is to the whole piece. Why, then, should a Christian be discontented when the title to his spiritual treasure remains? A thief may take away all the money I have about me, but not my land. Still a Christian has a title to the land of promise. Mary chose the better part, which could not be taken away.

2. Perhaps if your estate had not been lost, your soul would have been lost. Outward comforts often quench inward heat. God cannot bestow a jewel upon us but we fall so in love with it that we forget Him who gave it. What pity is it that we should commit idolatry with the creature! God is sometimes forced to drain away an estate. The silver and jewels are sometimes cast overboard to save the passenger. Many a man may curse the time that ever he had such an estate, when it has been an enchantment to draw away his heart from God.

There are some who would be rich, and they fall into a snare (1 Timothy 6:9). Are you troubled that God has prevented a snare? Riches are thorns, and are you angry that God has pulled away a thorn from you? Riches are compared to thick clay. Perhaps your affections, which are the feet of the soul, might have stuck so fast in this golden clay that they could not have ascended up to heaven. Be content. If God dams up our outward comfort, it is so that the stream of our love may run faster in another way.

3. If your estate is small, yet God can bless a little. It is not how much money we have, but how much blessing. He who often curses the bags of gold can bless the meal in the barrel and the oil in the jar. What if you do not have the full fleshpot? You still have a promise: "I will bless her provision" (Psalm 132:15), and then a little goes a long way. Be content; you have the dew of a blessing distilled. Where love is, a dinner of green herbs is sweet. I may add that, where the love of God is, afflictions are sweet. Another may have more estate than you, but more cares; more riches, but less rest; more revenues, but withal more occasions of expense. He has a greater inheritance, yet perhaps God does not give him power to eat thereof. He has the dominion of his estate, but not the use. He holds more, but enjoys less. In a word, you have less gold than he, and perhaps less guilt.

4. You never before thrived so in your spiritual trade. You heart was never so low as since your condition was low. You were never so poor in spirit, never so rich in faith. You never ran in the ways of God's commandments so fast as since some of your golden weights were taken off. You never had such trading for heaven in all your life. You never made such ventures upon the promise as since you left off your sea adventures. This is the best kind of merchandise. O Christian, you never had such income of the Spirit, such springtides of joy; and so what if you are

weak in estate if you are strong in assurance? Be content; what you have lost one way you have gained in another.

5. Be your material losses what they will, remember that in every loss there is only a suffering, but in every discontent there is a sin; and one sin is worse than a thousand sufferings. What? Because some of my revenues are gone, shall I part with some of my righteousness? Shall my faith and patience go, too? Because I do not possess an estate, shall I not, therefore, possess my own spirit? Oh, learn to be content!

APOLOGY 3. "It is sad with me in my relations. Where I should find the most comfort, there I have the most grief."

This objection branches itself into two particulars, to each of which I shall give a distinct reply.

1. "My child goes on in rebellion. I fear I have brought forth a child for the devil." It is sad, indeed, to think that hell should be paved with the skulls of any of our children; and certainly the pangs of grief which the mother has of this kind are worse than her pangs of travail. But though you ought to be humbled, yet you ought not be discontented, for consider:

You may pick something out of your child's undutifulness. The child's sin is sometimes the parent's sermon. The undutifulness of children to us may be a memento to put us in mind of our undutifulness to God. Time was when we were rebellious children. How long did our hearts stand out as garrisons against God? How long did He parley with us and beseech us before we would yield? He walked in the tenderness of His heart towards us, but we walked in the frowardness of our hearts towards Him; and since grace has been planted in our souls, how much of the wild olive is still in us! How many motions of the Spirit do we daily resist! How many unkindnesses and affronts have we put upon Christ! Let this open a spring of repentance; look upon your child's rebellion and mourn for your own rebellion.

Though to see him undutiful is your grief, it is not always your sin. Has a parent given the child not only the milk of the breast, but the sincere milk of the Word? Have you seasoned his tender years with religious education? You can do no more. Parents can only provide knowledge; God must work grace. They can only lay the wood together; it is God who must make it burn. A parent can only be a guide to show his child the way to heaven; the Spirit of God must be the lodestone to draw his heart in that way. "Am I in God's stead?" said Jacob. "Who has withheld the fruit of the womb?" (Genesis 30:2). Can I give children? If not, can a parent stand in God's stead to give grace? Who can help it if a child—having the light of conscience, Scripture, and education, these three torches in his hand—yet runs willfully into the deep ponds of sin? Weep for your child; pray for him; but do not sin for him by discontent.

Do not say that you have brought forth a child for the devil. God can restore him. He has promised to "turn the hearts of the children to their parents" (Malachi 4:6). When your child is going full sail to the devil, God can blow with a contrary wind of His Spirit and alter his course. When Paul was breathing out persecution against the saints and was sailing hellward, God turned him another way. He was going to Damascus, but God sent him to Ananias; before he was a persecutor, now he is a preacher. Though our children are, for the present, fallen into the devil's pound, God can turn them from the power of Satan (Acts 26:18), and bring them in at the twelfth hour. Monica was weeping for her son, Augustine. At last God brought him in upon prayer, and he became a famous instrument in the church of God.

2. The second branch of the objection is, "But my husband takes ill courses. Where I looked for honey, behold a sting."

It is sad to have the living and the dead tied together, yet let not your heart fret with discontent. Mourn for his sin, but do not murmur. For God has placed you in your relationship, and you cannot be discontented without quarreling with God. What? For every cross that befalls us, shall we call the infinite wisdom of God into question? Oh, the blasphemy of our hearts!

God can bring you gain by your husband's sin. Perhaps you would have never been so good if he had not been so bad. The fire burns hottest in the coldest climate. God often, by a divine contrast of circumstances, turns the sins of others to our good, and makes our maladies our medicines. The more profane the husband is, often the more holy the wife grows; the more earthly he is, the more heavenly she grows. God sometimes makes the husband's sin a spur to the wife's grace. His excesses are as a pair of bellows to blow up the flame of her zeal and devotion the more.

Is it not so? Does not your husband's wickedness send you to prayer? You, perhaps, would never have prayed so much if he had not sinned so much. His deadness quickens you all the more. The stone of his heart is a hammer to break your heart. The apostle said, "The unbelieving wife is sanctified by the believing husband" (1 Corinthians 7:14), but in this case: the believing wife is sanctified by the unbelieving husband in that she grows better. His sin is a whetstone to her grace and a medicine for her security.

APOLOGY 4. "But my friends have dealt very unkindly with me and proven to be false."
ANSWER. It is sad when a friend proves to be like a brook in summer. The traveler, being parched with heat, comes to the brook hoping to refresh himself, but the brook is dried up. Yet be content.
1. You are not alone; others of the saints have been betrayed by friends, and when they have leaned upon them they have been as a foot out of joint. This was true for David: "It was not an enemy reproaching me, but it was thou, a man my equal, my guide and my acquaintance; we took sweet counsel together" (Psalm 55:12–14). The antitype, Christ, was betrayed by a friend, and why should we think it strange to have the same measure dealt out to us as Jesus Christ had? The servant is not above his Master.
2. A Christian may often read his sin in his punishment. Has he not dealt treacherously with God? How often has he grieved the Comforter, broken his vows, and, through unbelief, sided with Satan against God! How often has he abused love, taking the jewels of God's mercies and making a golden calf of them, serving his own lusts! How often has he made the free grace of God, which should have been a bolt to keep out sin, rather a key to open the door to it! These wounds the Lord has received "in the house of a friend" (Zechariah 13:6). Look upon the unkindness of your friend and mourn for your own unkindness against God. Shall a Christian condemn that in another which he has been too guilty of himself?
3. Has your friend proved treacherous? Perhaps you depended too much on him, relied too heavily on him. If

you lay more weight upon a house than the pillars will bear, it must break. God said, "Trust ye not in a friend" (Micah 7:5). Perhaps you put more trust in him than you dared to put in God. Friends are as brittle glasses. We may use them, but if we lean too hard on them they will break. This is a matter that calls for humility, but not for sullenness and discontent.

4. You have a Friend in heaven who will never fail you. "There is a friend," said Solomon, "that sticketh closer than a brother" (Proverbs 18:24). Such a friend is God. He is very studious and inquisitive on our behalf. He considers with Himself, consults and projects how He may do us good. He is the best Friend, which fact may give contentment in the midst of all discourtesies from friends.

Consider that He is a loving Friend. God is love (1 John 4:16); hence He is said sometimes to engrave us on the palms of His hands (Isaiah 49:16) that we may never be out of His eye, and to carry us in His bosom (Isaiah 40:11) near His heart. There is no stop or break in His love, but, like the River Nile, it overflows all the banks. His love is as far beyond our thoughts as it is above our deserts. Oh, the infinite love of God in giving the Son of His love to be made flesh, which was more than if all the angels had been made worms! God, in giving Christ to us, gave His very heart to us. Here is love penciled out in all its glory, and engraved as with the point of a diamond. All other love is hatred in comparison to the love of our Friend.

He is a caring Friend. "He careth for you" (1 Peter 5:7). He minds and transacts our business as His own. He accounts His people's interests and contentments as His interests. He provides for us grace to enrich us and glory to ennoble us. David complained, "No man cared for my soul" (Psalm 142:4), but a Christian has a Friend who cares for him.

He is a prudent Friend. A friend may sometimes err through ignorance or mistake, and give his friend poison instead of sugar; but "God is wise in heart" (Job 9:4). He is skillfull as well as faithful. He knows what our disease is, and what medicine is most proper to apply. He knows what will do us good, and what wind will be best to carry us to heaven.

He is a faithful Friend. He is faithful in His promises. "In hope of eternal life, which God that cannot lie hath promised" (Titus 1:2). God's people are "children that will not lie" (Isaiah 63:8), but God is a God who cannot lie. He will not deceive the faith of His people; no, He cannot. He is called "the truth." He can as well cease to be God as cease to be true. The Lord may sometimes change His promise, as when He converts a temporal promise into a spiritual one, but He can never break a promise.

He is a compassionate Friend. Hence in Scripture we read of the yearning of His bowels (Jeremiah 31:20). God's friendship is nothing else but compassion, for there is naturally no affection in us to desire His friendship, nor goodness in us to deserve it. The magnet is in Himself. When we were full of blood, He was full of compassion. When we were enemies, He sent an ambassador of peace. When our hearts were turned away from God, His heart was turned towards us. Oh, the tenderness and sympathy of our Friend in heaven! We have some relentings of heart towards those who are in misery, but it is God who begets all the mercies and compassions that are in us; therefore He is called "the Father of mercies" (2 Corinthians 1:3).

He is a constant Friend. "His compassions fail not" (Lamentations 3:22). Friends often drop off as leaves in autumn during adversity. They are rather flatterers than friends, as Plutarch said. Joab was faithful to King David's house for a time, and did not follow after Absalom's treason, but within a while he proved false to the crown and went after the treason of Adonijah. God is a Friend forever. "Having loved His own, He loved them to the end" (John 13:1). What if I am despised? Yet God loves me. What if my friends cast me off? Yet God loves me. He loves to the end, and there is no end of that love.

This, I think, in cases of discourtesy and unkindness, is enough to charm down discontent.

APOLOGY 5. "I am under great reproaches."

Do not let this make you discontented, for:

1. It is a sign that there is some good in you. Socrates said, "What evil have I done that this bad man commends me for?" The applause of the wicked usually denotes some evil, and their censure imports some good. David wept and fasted, and that was turned to his reproach. As we must pass to heaven through the pikes of suffering, so through the clouds of reproach.

2. If your reproach is for God, as David's was ("for Thy sake I have borne reproach," Psalm 69:7), then it is rather a matter of triumph than rejection. Christ does not say, when you are reproached, "Be discontented," but He says, "Rejoice." Wear your reproach as a diadem of honor, for now "a spirit of glory rests upon you" (1 Peter 4:14). Put your reproaches into the inventory of your riches as did Moses (Hebrews 11:26). It should be a Christian's ambition to wear his Savior's livery, though it is sprinkled with blood and sullied with disgrace.

3. God will do us good by reproach, as David said of Shimei's cursing, "It may be that the Lord will requite me

good for his cursing this day" (2 Samuel 16:12). This puts us upon searching out sin. A child of God labors to read his sin in every stone of reproach that is cast at him. Besides, now we have an opportunity to exercise patience and humility.

4. Jesus Christ was content to be reproached for us. He despised not the shame of the cross (Hebrews 12:2). It may amaze us to think that He who was God could endure to be spit upon, to be crowned with thorns in a kind of jeer, and, when He was ready to bow His head upon the cross, to have the Jews wag their heads in scorn and say, "He saved others, Himself He cannot save." The shame of the cross was as much as the blood of the cross. His name was crucified before His body. The sharp arrows of reproach that the world shot at Christ went deeper into His heart than the spear. His sufferings were so ignominious that, as if the sun blushed to behold it, withdrew its bright beams and masked itself with a cloud (and well it might, when the Sun of righteousness was in an eclipse). All this humiliation and reproach the God of glory endured, or rather despised, for us. Oh, then, let us be content to have our names eclipsed for Christ! Let not reproach lie at our heart, but let us bind it as a crown about our head. Alas, what is reproach? This is but buckshot. How will men stand in the mouth of the cannon? Those who are discontent at a reproach will be offended at anything.

5. Is not many a man content to suffer reproach for maintaining his lust? Some glory in that which is their shame (Philippians 3:19); and shall we be ashamed of that which is our glory? Do not be troubled at these petty things; he whose heart is once divinely touched with the magnet of God's Spirit counts it his honor to be dishonored for Christ, and as much despises the world's censure

as he does its praise.

6. We live in an age where men dare to reproach God Himself. The divinity of the Son of God is blasphemously reproached by the Socinian. The blessed Bible is reproached by the Antiscripturist, as if it were but a legend of lies, and every man's faith a fable. The justice of God is called to the bar of reason by the Arminian. The wisdom of God in His providential acts is questioned by the atheist. The ordinances of God are decried by some as being too heavy a burden for a freeborn conscience, and too low and carnal for a sublime, seraphic spirit. The ways of God, which have the majesty of holiness shining in them, are calumniated by the profane. The mouths of men are open against God, as if He were a hard Master, and the path of religion too strict and severe. If man cannot give God a good word, shall we be discontented or troubled that they speak harshly of us? Such as labor to bury the glory of religion, shall we wonder that their throats are open sepulchres to bury our good name? Oh, let us be contented to have our names sullied a little while we are in God's scouring-house! The blacker we seem to be here, the brighter we shall shine when God sets us upon the celestial shelf.

APOLOGY 6. "I do not have the esteem from men as is suitable to my quality and graces." Does this trouble you? Consider:

1. The world is an unequal judge. As it is full of change, so of partiality. The world gives her respects as she does her places of preferment—more often by favor than merit. Do you have the ground of real worth in you? That is the best worth. Honor is in him who gives it. Better to deserve respect and not have it than to have it and not deserve it.

2. Do you have grace? God respects you, and His judgment is most worth prizing. A believer is a person of honor, being born of God. "Since thou wast precious in My sight, thou hast been honorable, and I have loved thee" (Isaiah 43:4). Let the world think what they will of you. Perhaps in their eyes you are a castaway, but in God's eyes a dove (Song of Solomon 2:14), a spouse (Song of Solomon 5:1), and a jewel (Malachi 3:17). Others account you the dregs and offscouring of the world, but God will give whole kingdoms for your ransom. Let this content you: "No matter with what oblique eyes I am looked upon in the world, God thinks well of me." It is better that God should approve than that man should applaud. The world may put us in its red letters, and God may put us in His black book. How is a man better when his fellow prisoners commend him, if his Judge condemns him? Oh, labor to keep in with God; prize His love! Let my fellow subjects frown; I am contented, being a favorite of the King of heaven.

3. If we are the children of God, we must look for disrespect. A believer is in the world, but not of the world. We are here in a pilgrim condition, out of our own country. Therefore, we must not look for the respect and acclamations of the world. It is sufficient that we shall have honor in our own country. It is dangerous to be the world's favorite.

4. Discontent arising from disrespect savors too much of pride. A humble Christian has a lower opinion of himself than others can have of him. He who is taken up about the thoughts of his sins and how he has provoked God cries out as Agur, "I am more brutish than any man" (Proverbs 30:2), and therefore is contented though he is set among the dogs of the flock. Though he is low in the

thoughts of others, yet he is thankful that he is not laid in the lowest hell. A proud man sets a high value upon himself, and is angry with others because they will not come up to his price. Take heed of pride. Oh, had others a window to look into your breast, or did your heart stand where your face does, you would wonder that you have as much respect as you do!

APOLOGY 7. "I meet with very great sufferings." Yet consider:

1. Your sufferings are not as great as your sins. Put these two in the balance and see which weighs heaviest. Where sin lies heavy, sufferings lie light. A carnal spirit makes more of his sufferings and less of his sins. He looks upon one with a broad perspective, but upon the other with a narrow perspective. The carnal heart cries out, "Take away the frogs," but a gracious heart cries, "Take away the iniquity." The one says, "Never has anyone suffered as I have done," but the other says, "Never has anyone sinned as I have done."

2. Are you under sufferings? You have an opportunity to show the valor and constancy of your mind. Some of God's saints would have accounted it a great favor to have been honored with martyrdom. One said, "I am in prison until I am in prison." You count that a trouble which others would have worn as a sign of their glory.

3. Even those who have gone only on moral principles have shown much constancy and contentment in their sufferings. Curtius, being bravely mounted and in armor, threw himself into a great gulf that the city of Rome might, according to the oracle, be delivered from the pestilence. We have a divine oracle that they who kill the body cannot hurt the soul; shall we not, with much con-

stancy and patience, devote ourselves to injuries for religion, and suffer for the truth rather than have the truth suffer for us? The Decii among the Romans vowed themselves to fight to the death that their legions and soldiers might be crowned with the honor of victory. Oh, what should we be content to suffer to make the truth victorious! Regulus, having sworn that he would return to Carthage (though he knew there was a furnace being heated for him there), yet, not daring to violate his oath, he ventured to go. We, then, who are Christians, having made a vow to Christ in baptism, and so often renewed it in the blessed sacrament, should, with much contentment, choose rather to suffer than violate our sacred oath. Thus, the blessed martyrs, with what courage and cheerfulness did they yield up their soul to God! And when the fire was set to their bodies, yet their spirits were not at all fired with passion or discontent. Though others hurt the body, let them not hurt the mind through discontent. Show by your heroic courage that you are above those troubles which you cannot be without.

APOLOGY 8. "But see how the wicked prosper!"
ANSWER. I confess that often the evil enjoy all the good and the good endure all the evil. David, though a good man, stumbled at this, and would likely have fallen. Well, be content, for remember:
1. These are not the only things, nor the best things. They are mercies outside the pale. These are but acorns with which God feeds swine. You who are believers have more choice fruit: the olive, the pomegranate, the fruit which grows on the true vine, Jesus Christ. Others have the fat of the earth; you have the dew of heaven. They have a swampland; you have those springs of living water

which are purified with Christ's blood and are sweetened with His love.

2. To see the wicked flourish is a matter of pity rather than envy. It is all the heaven they will have. "Woe to you rich men, for you have received your consolation" (Luke 6:24). Hence it is that David made it his prayer: "Deliver me from the wicked, from men of the world which have their portion in this life, and whose belly Thou fillest with Thy hid treasure" (Psalm 17:13–14). This was David's litany: "From men of the world who have their portion in this life, good Lord, deliver me." When the wicked have eaten their dainty dishes, there comes in a sad reckoning which will spoil all. The world is first musical, and then tragical. If you would have a man fry and blaze in hell, let him have enough of the fat of the earth. Oh remember, for every sand of mercy that runs out to the wicked, God puts a drop of wrath into his vial! Therefore, as that soldier said to his fellow, "Do you envy me my grapes? They cost me dearly; I must die for them." So, I say, do you envy the wicked? Alas, their prosperity is like Haman's banquet before his execution.

If a man were to be hanged, would one envy him to see him walk to the gallows through pleasant fields and fine galleries, or to see him go up the ladder in clothes of gold? The wicked may flourish in their finery for awhile, but when they flourish as the grass, it is that they shall be destroyed forever (Psalm 92:7). This proud grass shall be mowed down. Whatever a sinner enjoys, he has a curse with it; and shall we envy? What if poisoned bread is given to dogs? The long furrows in the backs of the godly have a seed of blessing in them, while the table of the wicked becomes a snare, and their honor their halter.

APOLOGY 9. "The times are full of heresy and impiety, and this is that which troubles me."

This apology consists of two branches:

1. "The times are full of heresy." This is sad, indeed. When the devil cannot destroy the church by violence, he endeavors to poison it. When he cannot set the corn on fire with Samson's fox tails, then he sows tares. As he labors to destroy the peace of the church by division, so he labors to destroy the truth of it by error. We may cry out with Seneca, "We live in times wherein there is a sluice open to all novel opinions, and every man's opinion is his Bible." Well, this may make us mourn, but do not let us murmur through discontent.

(1) Consider, error makes a discovery of men as follows:

Bad men. Error discovers such as are tainted and corrupt. When the leprosy broke forth in the forehead, then was the leper discovered. Error is a spiritual bastard: the devil is its father and pride its mother. You never knew any erroneous man but he was a proud man. Now it is good that such men are laid open for the purpose, first, that God's righteous judgments upon them may be adored; second, that others who are free do not get infected. If a man has the plague, it is well that it breaks forth. For my part, I would avoid a heretic as I would avoid the devil, for he is sent on his errand. I appeal to you, if there were a tavern in this city where, under pretense of selling wine, many hogsheads of poison were sold, would it not be good that others should know of it so that they may not buy it? It is good that those who have poisoned opinions should be known so that the people of God may not come near and taste of that poison.

Good men. Error is a touchstone to discover good men;

it tries the gold. "There must be heresies, that they which are approved may be made manifest" (1 Corinthians 11:19). Thus our love for Christ and our zeal for truth appears. God shows who are the living fish (those who are against the stream), who are the sound sheep (such as feed in the green pastures of the ordinances), and who are the doves (such as live in the best air where the Spirit breathes). God sets a garland of honor upon these: "These are they which escape out of great tribulation" (Revelation 7:14). So these are they who have opposed the errors of the times. These are they who have preserved the virginity of their conscience, who have kept their judgment sound and their heart soft. God will have a trophy of honor set upon some of His saints: they shall be renowned for their sincerity, being like the cypress, which keeps its greenness and freshness in the winter season.

(2) Do not be sinfully discontented, for God can make the errors of the church advantageous to the truth. Thus the truths of God have come to be more clearly confirmed. In law, when one man has laid a false title to a piece of land, the true title has, by this means, been all the more searched into and ratified. Some would never have studied as hard to defend the truth by Scripture if others had not endeavored to overthrow it by sophistry. All the mists and fogs of error that have risen out of the bottomless pit have made the glorious sun of truth shine so much the brighter. Had not Arius and Sabellius broached their damnable errors, the truth of those questions about the blessed Trinity would never have been so discussed and defended by Athanasius, Augustine, and others. Had not the devil brought in so much of his princely darkness, the champions for truth would never have run so fast to Scripture to light their lamps. So God, who has a wheel

within a wheel, watches over these things wisely, and turns them to the best.

(3) God raises the price of His truth all the more; the very shreds and filings of truth are venerable. When there is much counterfeit metal abroad, we prize true gold all the more. The pure wine of truth is never more precious than when unsound doctrines are broached and vented.

(4) Error makes us more thankful to God for the jewel of truth. When you see another infected with the plague, how thankful are you that God has freed you from the infection! When we see that others have leprosy of the head, how thankful are we to God that He has not given us over to believe a lie and so be damned! It is a good use even of the error of the times, when it makes us more humble and thankful, adoring the free grace of God who has kept us from drinking that deadly poison.

2. The second branch of this objection is the impiety of the times: "I live and converse among the profane. Oh, that I had wings like a dove that I might fly away and be at rest!"

It is sad, indeed, to be mixed with the wicked. David "beheld the transgressors and was grieved" (Psalm 119:158). Lot, who was a bright star in a dark night, was "vexed," or, as the word is in the original, "wearied out with the unclean conversation of the wicked" (2 Peter 2:7). He made the sins of Sodom spears that pierced his own soul. We ought, if there is any spark of divine love in us, to be very sensible of the sins of others, and to have our hearts bleed for them. Yet let us not break forth in murmuring or discontent, knowing that God, in His Providence, has permitted it, and surely not without some reasons, for:

(1) The Lord makes the wicked a hedge to defend the godly. The wise God often makes those who are wicked and peaceable a means to safeguard His people from those who are wicked and cruel. The king of Babylon kept Jeremiah, and gave special order for his care so that he lacked nothing. God sometimes causes brazen sinners to be brazen walls to defend His people.

(2) God interweaves and mingles the wicked with the godly so that the godly may be a means to save the wicked. Such is the beauty of holiness that it has a magnetic force in it to allure and draw even the wicked. Sometimes God makes a believing husband a means to convert an unbelieving wife, and vice versa. "What knowest thou, O wife, whether thou shalt save thy husband? or how knowest thou, O man, whether thou shalt save thy wife?" (1 Corinthians 7:16). The godly who live among the wicked, by their prudent advice and pious example, have won them to embrace religion. If there were not some godly among the wicked, how in a probable way, without a miracle, can we expect that the wicked should be converted? Those who are now shining saints in heaven sometimes served divers lusts. Paul was once a persecutor, Augustine once a Manichee, Luther once a monk; but by the severe and holy carriage of the godly they were converted to the faith.

APOLOGY 10. "I cannot," says the Christian, "discourse with that fluency, nor pray with that elegance, as others."

ANSWER. Grace is beyond gifts. You compare your grace with another's gifts. There is a vast difference. Grace without gifts is infinitely better than gifts without grace. In religion, the vitals are best. Gifts are a more extrinsic and

common work of the Spirit, which is incidental to reprobates. Grace is a more distinguishing work, and is a jewel
hung only upon the elect. Do you have the seed of God,
the holy anointing? Be content.

You say you cannot discourse with the fluency that
others have, but religious experiences are beyond notions
and impressions are beyond expressions. Judas, no doubt,
could make a learned discourse of Christ, but the woman
in Luke 8:47, who felt virtue coming out of Him, fared
better. A sanctified heart is better than a silver tongue.
There is as much difference between gifts and grace as between a tulip painted on the wall and one growing in the
garden.

You say you cannot not pray with the elegance that
others have, but prayer is a matter more of the heart than
of the head. In prayer, it is not so much fluency that prevails as fervency. Nor is God so much taken with the elegance of speech as with the efficacy of the Spirit. Humility
is better than volubility. Here the mourner is the orator;
sighs and groans are the best rhetoric.

Be not discontented, for God usually proportions a
man's parts to the place where He calls him. Some are set
in a higher sphere and function; their place requires
more parts and abilities. But the most inferior member is
useful in his place and shall have a power delegated for
the discharge of his peculiar office.

APOLOGY 11. "Alas, my disquiet and discontent are
not so much for myself as for the church. The Church of
God suffers."

ANSWER. I confess it is sad, and we ought for this "to
hang our harps upon the willows" (Psalm 137:2). He is a
wooden leg in Christ's body who is not sensible of the

state of the body. As a Christian must not be proud flesh, so neither should he be dead flesh. When the church of God suffers he must sympathize. Jeremiah wept for the virgin daughter of Zion. We must feel our brethren's hard cords through our soft beds. In music, if one string is touched all the rest sound. When God strikes upon our brethren, "our bowels must sound as a harp" (Isaiah 16:11). Be sensitive, but do not give way to discontent, for consider:

God sits at the stern of His Church. Sometimes it is as a ship tossed upon the waves ("O thou afflicted and tossed," Isaiah 54:11), but cannot God bring this ship to haven though it meets with a storm upon the sea?

The ship in the gospel was tossed because sin was in it, but it was not overwhelmed because Christ was in it. Christ is in the ship of His Church; do not fear sinking. The church's anchor is cast in heaven. Do we not think that God loves His Church, and takes as much care of it as we can? The names of the twelve tribes were on Aaron's breast, signifying how near to God's heart His people are. They are His portion, and shall that be lost? They are His glory, and shall that be finally eclipsed? No, certainly. God can deliver His Church not only from, but by opposition. The Church's pangs shall help forward her deliverance.

God has always propagated religion by sufferings. The foundation of the Church has been laid in blood, and these sanguine showers have ever made it more fruitful. Cain put the knife to Abel's throat, and ever since the Church's veins have bled; but she is like the vine which, by bleeding, grows. She is like the palm tree: the more weight is laid upon it, the higher it rises. The holiness and patience of the saints under their persecution have added to both the growth and crown of religion.

Basil and Tertullian observe of the primitive martyrs that many of the heathens, seeing their zeal and constancy, turned Christian. Religion is that phoenix which has always revived and flourished in the ashes of holy men. Isaiah was sawed asunder; Peter was crucified at Jerusalem upside down; Cyprian, Bishop of Carthage, and Polycarp of Smyrna were both martyred for religion. Yes, evermore the truth has been sealed by blood and gloriously dispersed. Julian refrained from persecuting not out of piety, but out of envy, because the church grew so fast and multiplied, as Nazianzus well observes.

APOLOGY 12. "It is not my trouble that troubles me, but it is my sins that disquiet me and make me discontented."

ANSWER. Be sure it is so. Do not prevaricate with God and your own soul. In true mourning for sin, when the present suffering is removed, yet the sorrow is not removed. But suppose the apology is real and sin is the ground of your discontent; nevertheless, I answer, a man's disquiet about sin may be beyond its bounds in these three cases:

1. When it is disheartening, that is, when it sets up sin above mercy. If Israel had only dwelt upon its sting and not looked up to the brazen serpent, the people would never have been healed. That sorrow for sin which drives us away from God is not without sin, for there is more despair in it than remorse. The soul has so many tears in its eyes that it cannot see Christ. Sorrow in itself does not save (that would be to make a Christ of our tears), but it is useful as it is preparatory in the soul, making sin vile and Christ precious. Oh, look up to the brazen Serpent, the Lord Jesus! A sight of His blood will revive; the medicine

of His merits is broader than our sore.

It is Satan's policy either to keep us from seeing our sins or, if we must see them, to see that we are swallowed up by sorrow. Either he will stupefy us or frighten us. He will either keep the glass of the law from our eyes, or else pencil out our sins in such crimson colors that we may sink in the quicksands of despair.

2. When sorrow is indisposing, it makes the heart out of tune for prayer, meditation, and holy conference. It secludes the soul. This is not sorrow, but rather sullenness, and renders a man not so much penitential as cynical.

3. When it is out of season. God bids us rejoice, and we hang our harps upon the willows. He bids us trust, and we cast ourselves down, and are brought even to the margin of despair. If Satan cannot keep us from mourning, he will be sure to put us upon it when it is least in season.

When God calls us in a special manner to be thankful for mercy and put on our white robes, then Satan will be putting us into mourning, and, instead of a garment of praise, will clothe us with a spirit of heaviness. So God loses the acknowledgment of a mercy, and we lose the comfort.

If your sorrow has tuned and fitted you for Christ—if it has raised in you high prizings of Him, strong hungerings after Him, sweet delight in Him—this is as much as God requires. A Christian only sins further if he vexes and tortures himself upon the rack of his own discontent.

And thus I hope I have answered the most material objections and apologies which this sin of discontent makes for itself. I see no reason why a Christian should be discontented, unless it is for his discontent.

Chapter 11

Divine Motives to Contentment

I proceed to the arguments or motives that may quicken to contentment:

ARGUMENT 1. Consider the excellency of it. Contentment is a flower that does not grow in every garden. It teaches a man how to abound in the midst of want. You would think it was excellent if I could prescribe a remedy or antidote against poverty, but behold, here is that which is more excellent. For a man to want and yet have enough—this only comes through contentment of spirit. Contentment is a remedy against all our troubles, a comfort to all our burdens; it is the cure of care. Contentment, though it is not properly a grace (it is rather a disposition of mind), yet has in it a happy mixture of all the graces. It is a most precious compound which is made up of faith, patience, meekness, and humility, which are the ingredients put into it. Now there are these seven rare excellencies in contentment:

1. A contented Christian carries heaven with him. For what is heaven but that sweet repose and full contentment that the soul shall have in God? In contentment there are the first fruits of heaven. There are two things in a contented spirit which make it like heaven.

First, God is there. Something of God is to be seen in that heart. A discontented Christian is like a rough, tempestuous sea. When the water is rough, you can see nothing there; but when it is smooth and serene, then you may behold your face in the water. When the heart rages through discontent, it is like a rough sea. You can see nothing there but passion and murmuring. There is nothing of God, nothing of heaven in that heart. But by virtue of contentment, it is like the sea when it is smooth and calm. There is a shining face there. You may see something of Christ in that heart, a representation of all the graces.

Second, rest is there. Oh, what a Sabbath is kept in a contented heart! What a heaven! A contented Christian is like Noah in the ark: though the ark was tossed with waves, Noah could sit and sing in the ark. The soul that has gotten into the ark of contentment sits quietly and sails above all the waves of trouble. He can sing in this spiritual ark. The wheels of the chariot move, but the axle stirs not. The circumference of the heavens is carried about the earth, but the earth does not move out of its center. When we meet with motion and change in the creatures round about us, a contented spirit is not stirred or moved out of its center. The sails of a mill move with the wind, but the mill itself stands still, an emblem of contentment. When our outward estate moves with the wind of Providence, yet the heart is settled through holy contentment; and when others are like quicksilver, shaking and trembling through disquiet, the contented spirit can say with David, "O God, my heart is fixed, my heart is fixed" (Psalm 57:7). What is this but a piece of heaven?

2. Whatever is defective in the creature is made up in contentment. A Christian may lack the comforts that others have, the land and possessions, but God has distilled into his heart that contentment which is far better. In this sense what our Savior said is true: "He shall have in this life a hundredfold" (Matthew 19:29). Perhaps he who ven-

tures all for Christ never has his house or land again, but God gives him a contented spirit; and this breeds such joy in the soul as is infinitely sweeter than all his houses or lands which he left for Christ.

It was sad with David regarding his outward comforts. He was being driven, as some think, from his kingdom, yet, in regard to that sweet contentment he found in God, he had more comfort than men normally have in time of harvest and vintage (Psalm 4:7). One man has a house and lands to live upon; another has nothing but a small trade, yet even that brings in a livelihood. A Christian may have little in the world, but he drives the trade of contentment; and so he knows how to want as well as how to abound. Oh, the rare art and miracle of contentment! Wicked men are often disquieted in the enjoyment of all things. The contented Christian is well amidst the want of all things.

QUESTION. But how does a Christian come to be contented in the deficiency of outward comforts?

ANSWER. A Christian finds contentment distilled out of the breasts of the promises. He is poor in purse, but rich in promise. There is one promise that brings much sweet contentment into the soul: "They that seek the Lord shall not want any good thlng" (Psalm 34:10). If the thing we desire is good for us, we shall have it. If it is not good, then not having it is good for us. Resting satisfied with this promise gives contentment.

3. Contentment makes a man in tune to serve God. It oils the wheels of the soul and makes it more agile and nimble. It composes the heart and is now fit for prayer, meditation, and the like. How can he who is in a passion of grief or discontent "serve God without distraction" (1 Corinthians 7:35)? Contentment prepares and tunes

the heart. First you prepare the violin and wind up the strings before you play a piece of music. When a Christian's heart is wound up to this heavenly frame of contentment, then it is fit for duty. A discontented Christian is like Saul when the evil spirit came upon him. Oh, what jarrings and discords he made in prayer! When an army is put into disorder, it is not fit for battle. When the thoughts are scattered and distracted about the cares of life, a man is not fit for devotion. Discontent takes the heart wholly off from God and fixes it upon the present trouble, so that a man's mind is not upon his prayer, but upon his cross.

Discontent disjoints the soul, and it is impossible now that a Christian should go steadily and cheerfully in God's service. Oh, how lame is his devotion! The discontented person gives God but half a duty; his religion is nothing but bodily exercise, and lacks a soul to animate it. David would not offer to God that which cost him nothing (2 Samuel 24:24). Where there is too much worldly care, there is too little spiritual cost in a duty. The discontented person does his duty by halves. He is just like Ephraim, a cake not turned (Hosea 7:8). He is a cake baked on one side. He gives God the outside, but not the spiritual part. His heart is not in duty. He is baked on one side, but the other side is dough; and what profit is there in such raw, undigested services? He who gives God only the skin of worship, what can he expect more than the shell of comfort? Contentment brings the heart into frame, and only then do we give God the flower and spirits of a duty, when the soul is composed. A Christian's heart is then intense and serious.

There are some duties which we cannot perform as we ought without contentment:

• To rejoice in God. How can he rejoice who is discontented? He is more fit for repining than rejoicing.

• To be thankful for mercy. Can a discontented person be thankful? He can be fretful, not thankful.

• To justify God in His proceedings. How can he do this who is discontented with his condition? He will sooner censure God's wisdom than clear His justice. Oh, then, how excellent is contentment, which prepares and, as it were, strings the heart for duty! Indeed, contentment not only makes our duties lively and agile, but acceptable. It is this that puts beauty and worth into them, for contentment settles the soul. When milk is always stirring, you can make nothing of it, but let it settle awhile and then it turns to cream. In the same way, when the heart is overly stirred with disquiet and discontent, you can make nothing of those duties. How thin, how flat, how dull are they! But when the heart is once settled by holy contentment, now there is some worth in our duties, now they turn to cream.

4. Contentment is the spiritual arch or pillar of the soul. It fits a man to bear burdens. He whose heart is ready to sink under the least sin has, by virtue of this contentment, an invincible spirit under sufferings. A contented Christian is like the camomile: the more it is trodden upon, the more it grows. As medicine works diseases out of the body, so contentment works trouble out of the heart. It argues, "If I am under reproach, God can vindicate me. If I am in want, God can relieve me." 2 Kings 3:17: "Ye shall not see wind nor rain, yet the valley shall be filled with water." Thus holy contentment keeps the heart from fainting.

In the autumn, when the fruit and leaves are blown off, there is still sap in the root. When there is an autumn upon our eternal felicity, the leaves of our estate drop off, but still there is the sap of eternal contentment in the heart, and a Christian has life inwardly when his outward comforts do not blossom. The contented heart is never out of heart. Contentment is like a golden shield that beats back discouragements. Humility is like the lead in the net, which keeps the soul down when it is rising through passion; and contentment is like the cork which keeps the heart up when it is sinking through discouragement. Contentment is the great support; it is like the beam which bears whatever weight is laid upon it. No, it is like a rock that breaks the waves.

It is strange to observe the same affliction lying upon two men, and how differently they carry themselves under it. The contented Christian is like Samson, who carried away the gates of the city upon his back (Judges 16:3). He can go away with his cross cheerfully and make nothing of it. The other is like Issachar couching down under his burden (Genesis 49:14). The reason is that one is content, and that breeds courage, while the other is discontented, and that breeds fainting. Discontent swells the grief, and grief breaks the heart. When this sacred sinew of contentment begins to shrink, we go limping under our afflictions. We do not know what burdens God may exercise us with; let us therefore preserve contentment. As is our contentment, such will be our courage. David, with his five stones and his sling, defied Goliath and overcame him. Get contentment into the sling of your heart, and with this sacred stone you may both defy the world and conquer it. You may break those afflictions which otherwise will break you.

5. Contentment prevents many sins and temptations. First, it prevents many sins. Where there is a lack of con-

tentment, there is no lack of sin. Discontentedness with
our condition is a sin that does not go alone, but is like
the first link of a chain which draws all the other links
along with it. In particular, contentment prevents two sins:

Impatience. Discontent and impatience are two twins.
"This evil is of the Lord; why should I wait any longer?"
(2 Kings 6:33)—as if God were so tied that He must give
us the mercy just when we desire it. Impatience is no small
sin, as will appear if you consider how it arises.

It arises from lack of faith. Faith gives a right notion of
God. It is an intelligent grace; it believes that God's wisdom tempers, and His love sweetens, all ingredients. This
works patience. "Shall I not drink the cup which My
Father hath given Me?" Impatience is the daughter of in-
fidelity. If a patient has a bad opinion of the physician,
and thinks that he has come to poison him, he will take
none of his medicines. When we have a prejudice against
God, and imagine that He comes to kill and undo us, then
we storm and cry out through impatience. We are like a
foolish man, to use Chrysostom's simile, who cries out,
"Away with the plaster, though it is in order to be a cure."
Is it not better that the plaster smart a little than that the
wound fester and rankle?

Impatience comes from lack of love to God. We will
bear the reproofs of him whom we love not only patiently,
but thankfully. "Love thinks no evil" (1 Corinthians 13:5).
It puts the fairest and most candid gloss upon the actions
of a friend. Love covers evil. If it were possible for God in
the least manner to err (which would be blasphemy to
think), love would cover that error. Love takes everything
in the best sense; it makes us bear any stroke; it endures
all things (1 Corinthians 13:7). Had we love to God, we
would have patience.

Impatience comes from lack of humility. The impatient man was never humbled under the burden of sin. He who studies his sins—the numberless number of them, how they are twisted together and sadly accented—is patient and says, "I will bear the indignation of the Lord, because I have sinned against Him" (Micah 7:9). The greater noise drowns the lesser. When the sea roars, the rivers are still. He who lets his thoughts wander on his sin is both silent and amazed; he wonders that it is no worse with him. How great, then, is this sin of impatience! And how excellent is contentment (which is a counterpoison against this sin)! The contented Christian, believing that God does all in love, is patient, and has not one word to say unless it is to justify God. That is the first sin which contentment prevents.

Murmuring. Contentment prevents murmuring, a sin which is a degree higher than the other. Murmuring is quarreling with God, and protesting bitterly against Him. "They spake against God" (Numbers 21:5). The murmurer says that God has not dealt well with him, and that he has deserved better from Him. The murmurer charges God with folly. This is the language, or rather the blasphemy, of a murmuring spirit: "God might have been a wiser and a better God." The murmurer is a mutineer. The Israelites are called both murmurers and rebels in Numbers 17:10, and is not rebellion as the sin of witchcraft? You who are a murmurer are, in God's account, like a witch, a sorcerer, as one who deals with the devil. This is a sin of the first magnitude. Murmuring often ends in cursing. Micah's mother fell to cursing when the talents of silver were taken away (Judges 17:2). So does the murmurer when a part of his estate is taken away. Our murmuring is the devil's music. This is that sin which God cannot bear: "How long shall I bear with this congregation that murmurs against Me?" (Numbers 14:27). It is a sin which whets the sword against a people; it is a land-destroying sin. "Murmur ye not as some of them also murmured, and were destroyed by the destroyer" (1 Corinthians 10:10). It is a ripening sin which, without God's mercy, will hasten England's funerals. Oh, then, how excellent is contentment, which prevents this sin! To be contented and yet murmur is an impossibility. A contented Christian acquiesces in his present condition and does not murmur, but admires. Herein appears the excellency of contentment: it is a spiritual antidote against sin.

Contentment also prevents many temptations. Discontent is a devil that is always tempting. It puts a man upon indirect means. He who is poor and discontent will attempt anything. He will go to the devil for riches. He who is proud and discontented will hang himself, as Ahitophel did when his counsel was rejected. Satan takes great advantage of our discontent. He loves to fish in these troubled waters.

Discontent both eclipses reason and weakens faith. It is Satan's usual policy to break over the hedge where it is weakest. Discontent makes a breach in the soul, and usually at this breach the devil enters in by a temptation and storms the soul. How easily can the devil, by his logic, dispute a discontented Christian into sin! He forms such a syllogism as this: "He who is in want must study self-preservation. But you are now in want; therefore you ought to study self-preservation." Hereupon, to make good his conclusion, he tempts to the forbidden fruit, not distinguishing between what is needful and what is lawful. "What?" he says, "do you lack a livelihood? Never be such a fool as to starve. Take the rising side at a venture. Be it good or bad, eat the bread of deceit; drink the wine of violence." Thus you see how the discontented man is a prey to that sad temptation to steal and to take God's name in vain.

Contentment is a shield against temptation, for he who is content knows as well how to want as how to abound. He will not sin to get a living. Though the bill of fare grows short, he is content. He lives as the birds of the air, upon God's providence, and doubts not but that he shall have enough to pay for his passage to heaven.

Discontent tempts a man to atheism and apostasy. "Surely there is no God to take care of things here below. Would He suffer them to be in want who have walked mournfully before Him?" says discontent. "Throw off Christ's livery; desist from your religion." Thus Job's wife, being discontented with her condition, said to her husband, "Dost thou still retain thy integrity?" (Job 2:9). It is as if she had said, "Do you not see, Job, what has become of all your religion? You fear God and eschew evil; and how are you the better for it? See how God turns His hand against you. He has smitten you in your body, estate, and relations; and do you still retain your integrity? What, still devout? Still weep and pray before Him? You fool, cast off religion and turn atheist!"

Here was a sore temptation the devil handed over to Job by his discontented wife. Only his grace, as a golden shield, warded off the blow from his heart. "Thou speakest as one of the foolish women" (Job 2:10). The discontented person says, "What profit is it to serve the Almighty? Those who never trouble themselves about religion are the prosperous men, and I, in the meantime, suffer want. I might as well give over driving the trade of religion if this is all my reward." This is a sore temptation, and it often prevails. Atheism is the fruit that grows out of the blossom of discontent.

Oh, then, behold the excellency of contentment! It repels this temptation. "If God is mine," says the contented spirit, "it is enough. Though I have no lands or tenements, His smile makes it heaven. His love is better than wine. Better are the grapes of Ephraim than the vintage of Abiezer (Judges 8:2). I have little in hand, but much in hope. My livelihood is short, but this is His promise: eternal life. I am pursued by malice, but better is persecuted godliness than prosperous wickedness." Thus, divine contentment is a spiritual antidote against both sin and temptation.

6. Contentment sweetens every condition. As Christ turned the water into wine, so contentment turns the waters of Marah into spiritual wine. Have I but little? Yet it is more than I can deserve or claim. This modest amount is given in mercy; it is the fruit of Christ's blood. It is the legacy of free grace. A small present sent from a king is highly valued. This little I have is with a good conscience. It is not stolen water. Guilt has not muddied or poisoned it; it runs pure. This little is a pledge of more. This bit of bread is an earnest of that bread which I shall eat in the kingdom of God. This little water in the jar is an earnest of that heavenly nectar which shall be distilled from the true Vine. Do I meet with some crosses? If they are heavy, my comfort is that I do not have far to go. I shall but carry my cross to Golgotha, and there I shall leave it. My cross is light in regard to the weight of glory. Has God taken away my comforts from me? It is well, the Comforter still abides.

Thus contentment, as a honeycomb, drops sweetness into every condition. But discontent is a leaven that sours every comfort. It puts aloes and wormwood upon the breast of the creature. It lessens every mercy and triples every cross, but the contented spirit sucks sweetness from every flower of Providence. It can make something sweet out of poison. Contentment is full of consolation.

7. Contentment has this excellency: it is the best commentator upon Providence. It makes a fair interpretation of all God's dealings. Let the providences of God be never so dark or bloody, contentment always construes them in the best sense. I may say of it as the apostle said of charity, "It thinks no evil" (1 Corinthians 13:5). Sickness, says contentment, is God's furnace to refine His gold and make it sparkle all the more. The prison is an oratory, or house of prayer. What if God melts away the creature from me? He saw, perhaps, that my heart grew too much in love with them. Had I been long in that fat pasture, I would have indulged myself to excess; and the better my estate had been, the worse my soul would have been. God is wise. He has done this either to prevent some sin or to exercise some grace. What a blessed frame of heart is this!

A contented Christian is an advocate for God against unbelief and impatience, whereas discontent takes everything from God in the worst sense; it accuses and censures God: "This evil I feel is but a symptom of a greater evil; God is about to undo me." "The Lord hath brought us hither into the wilderness to slay us" (Numbers 20:4). The contented soul takes all well, and when his condition is never so bad he can say, "Yet God is good" (Psalm 73:1).

ARGUMENT 2. A Christian has that which may make him content.

1. Has not God given you Christ? In Him there are unsearchable riches. He is such a gold mine of wisdom and grace that all the saints and angels can never dig to the bottom. As Seneca said to his friend Polybius, "Never

complain of your hard fortune as long as Caesar is your friend," so I say to a believer, "Never complain as long as Christ is your Friend." He is an enriching pearl, a sparkling diamond. The infinite luster of His merits makes us shine in God's eyes. In Him there is both fullness and sweetness; He is indescribable good. Lift up your thoughts to the highest pinnacle; stretch them to the utmost; let them wander to their full latitude and extent—yet they fall infinitely short of those ineffable and inexhaustible treasures which are locked up in Jesus Christ. And is there not enough here to give the soul contentment? A Christian who lacks necessities, yet, having Christ, has the one thing needful.

2. Your soul is exercised and enameled with the graces of the Spirit, and is this not enough to give contentment? Grace is of a divine birth; it is the new plantation; it is the flower of the heavenly paradise; it is the embroidery of the Spirit; it is the seed of God; it is the sacred unction; it is Christ's portrait in the soul; it is the very foundation on which the superstructure of glory is laid. Oh, of what infinite value is grace! What a jewel is faith! Well may it be called "precious faith" (2 Peter 1:1). What is love but a divine sparkle in the soul? A soul beautified with grace is like a room richly hung with tapestries or the firmament bespangled with glittering stars. These are the true riches; and is not there enough here to give the soul contentment? What are all other things but like the wings of a butterfly—curiously painted, they defile our fingers.

Earthly riches, Augustine said, are full of poverty. So, indeed, they are, for they cannot enrich the soul. Oftentimes, under silken apparel, there is a thread-bare soul. Also, earthly riches are corruptible. "Riches are not forever," as the wise man said in Proverbs 27:4. Heaven is a place where gold and silver will not go. A believer is rich towards God; why, then, are you discontented? Has not God given you that which is better than the world? So what if He does not give you the box, if He gives you the jewel? So what if He denies you farthings, if He gives you a better coin? He gives you gold: spiritual mercies. What if the water in the bottle is spent? You have enough in the Fountain. What need does he have to complain of the world's emptiness who has God's fullness? "The Lord is my portion," said David in Psalm 16:5. Then let the lines fall where they will, in a sickbed or a prison. I will say, "The lines are fallen unto me in pleasant places; yea, I have a goodly heritage."

Are you not heir to all the promises? Do you not have a foretaste of heaven? When you let go your hold of natural life, are you not sure of eternal life? Has God not given you the earnest and first fruits of glory? Is not this enough to spur the heart to contentment?

> What if some have a cargo of cloves and
>   nutmegs, and in cinnamon sail?
> If thou hast wherewithal
> To spice a draught when griefs prevail,
> And for the future time art heir
> To th' Isle of Spices, is it not fair?
>   (Herbert's *Poems*)

ARGUMENT 3. Be content or else you refute your own prayers.

We pray, "Thy will be done." It is the will of God that we should be in such a condition. He has decreed it and He sees it to best for us. Why, then, do we murmur, and why are we discontented with what we pray for? Either we are not in good earnest in our prayer, which argues hypocrisy, or else we contradict ourselves, which argues folly.

ARGUMENT 4. God now has His end and Satan misses his end.

1. God has His end. God's end in all His cross providences is to bring the heart to submit and be content. And, indeed, this pleases God much. He loves to see His children satisfied with that portion He carves and allots them. It contents Him to see us content. Therefore, let us acquiesce in God's providence; for now God has His end.

2. Satan misses his end. The end why the devil, though by God's permission, smote Job in his body and estate was to perplex his mind. He vexed his body on purpose that he might disquiet his spirit. He hoped to bring Job into a fit of discontent, and that Job, in a passion, would then break forth against God. But Job, being so well contented with his condition, fell to blessing God and disappointed Satan of his hope.

Revelation 2:10 says, "The devil shall cast some of you into prison." Why does the devil throw us into prison? It is not so much to hurt our body as to molest our mind. He would imprison our contentment and disturb the regular motion of our souls; this is his design. It is not so much to put us into a prison as to put us into a passion that he attempts. But by our holy contentment, Satan loses his prey and misses his end.

The devil has often deceived us. The best way to deceive him is by contentment in the midst of temptation. Our contentment will discontent Satan. Oh, let us not gratify our enemy! Discontent is the devil's delight. Now it is as he would have it; he loves to warm himself at the fire of our passions. Repentance is the joy of the angels, and discontent is the joy of the devils. As the devil dances at discord, so he sings at discontent. The fire of our passions makes for the devil a bonfire. It is a kind of heaven to him to see us torturing ourselves with our own troubles; but by holy contentment we frustrate him of his purpose and, as it were, put him out of countenance.

ARGUMENT 5. By contentment a Christian gets a victory over himself. When a man is able to rule his own spirit, this of all others is the most noble conquest. Passion denotes weakness. To be discontented is suitable to flesh and blood, but to be in every state content? To be reproached, yet content? Imprisoned, yet content? This is above nature. This is some of that holy valor and chivalry which only a divine Spirit is able to infuse. To be patient in the midst of affronts of this world, and in the changes of the world to have the spirit calmed? This is a conquest worthy, indeed, of the garland of honor. Holy Job divested and gave up all, leaving his scarlet and embracing his dunghill; it was a sad catastrophe, yet he had learned contentment. It is said that he fell upon the ground and worshipped (Job 1:20). One would have thought he would have fallen on the ground and blasphemed. No, he fell and worshipped; he adored God's justice and holiness. Behold the strength of grace! Here was a humble submission, yet a noble conquest. He got the victory over himself. It is no great matter for a man to yield to his own passions (this is facile and feminine), but to content himself in denying himself is sacred.

ARGUMENT 6. The sixth argument to spur the heart to contentment is the consideration that all God's providences, however cross or bloody, shall do a believer good. "And we know that all things work together for good to them that love God" (Romans 8:28). Not only all good things, but all evil things work for good; and shall we be

discontented with that which works for our good?
Suppose our troubles are twisted together and sadly accented, as the poet Ovid describes it:

> As many mussel-shells as the seashores have,
> As many flowers as the pleasant rose-gardens
>   have,
> As many seeds as the sleep-inducing poppy has,
> As many wild beasts as the forest nourishes,
> With as many fishes as the tide is overflowing,
> And with as many feathers as the bird beats
>   the soft air,
> With as many adversities am I burdened.

What if sickness, poverty, reproach, and lawsuits unite and muster their forces against us? All shall work for good. Our maladies shall be our medicines; and shall we repine at that which shall undoubtedly do us good? "Unto the upright there ariseth light in darkness" (Psalm 112:4). Affliction may be baptized Marah: it is bitter, but healthful. Because this point is so full of comfort, and may be a most excellent panacea against discontent, I shall wander a little.

QUESTION. How do the evils of affliction work for good?

ANSWER. In several ways. They are disciplinary; they teach us. The psalmist, having very elegantly described the church's trouble in Psalm 74, prefixes a title to the psalm which identifies it as a psalm giving instruction. That which seals up instruction works for good. God sometimes puts us under the black rod, but it is a rod of discipline. "Hear ye the rod, and who hath appointed it" (Micah 6:9). God makes our adversity our university. Affliction is a preacher. "Blow the trumpet in Tekoa" (Jeremiah 6:1).

The trumpet was to preach to the people, as appears in verse 8: "Be thou instructed, O Jerusalem." Sometimes God speaks to the minister to lift up his voice like a trumpeter (Isaiah 58:1); here He speaks to the trumpet to lift up its voice like a minister.

Afflictions teach us humility. We are commonly prosperous and proud. Corrections are God's corrosives to eat out the proud flesh. Jesus Christ is a "lily of the valleys" (Song of Solomon 2:1). He dwells in a humble heart. God brings us into the valley of tears that He may bring us into the valley of humility. "Remembering my affliction, the wormwood and the gall, my soul hath them still in remembrance, and is humbled in me" (Lamentations 3:19–20).

When men are grown high, God has no better way with them than to brew them a cup of wormwood. Afflictions are compared to thorns. God's thorns are to prick the bladder of pride. Suppose a man runs at another with a sword and wounds him, but only so as to cut out his abscess; this does him good. God's sword is to let out the abscess of pride; and shall that which makes us humble make us discontented?

Afflictions teach us repentance. "Thou hast chastised me, and I was chastised. I repented, and after I was instructed I smote upon my thigh" (Jeremiah 31:18–19). Repentance is the precious fruit that grows upon the cross. When the fire is put under the still, the water drops from the roses. Fiery afflictions make the waters of repentance drop and distill from the eyes; and is here any cause of discontent?

Afflictions teach us to pray better. "They poured out a prayer when Thy chastening was upon them" (Isaiah 26:16). Before they would say a prayer; now they poured

out a prayer. Jonah was asleep in the ship, but awake and
in prayer in the whale's belly. When God puts us under
the firebrands of affliction, now our hearts boil over all
the more. God loves to have His children possessed with a
spirit of prayer. Never did David, the sweet singer of Israel,
tune his harp more melodiously; never did he pray better
than when he was upon the waters. Thus, afflictions do us
good; and shall we be discontented at that which is for our
good?

Afflictions serve to prove us. Gold is not the worse for
being tried, or corn for being fanned. Affliction is the
touchstone of sincerity to see what metal we are made of.
Affliction is God's fan and His sieve. It is good that men's
motives be known. Some serve God for a livery. They are
like the fisherman who makes use of his net only to catch
the fish; they go fishing with the net of religion only to
catch preferment. Affliction reveals these men. The
Donatists went to the Goths when the Arians prevailed.
Hypocrites will not sail in a storm. True grace holds out in
the winter season. That is a precious faith which, like the
star, shines brightest in the darkest night. It is good that
our graces should be brought to a trial. Thus we have the
comfort and the gospel has the honor; and why, then, are
we discontented?

Afflictions purge us. These evils work for good because
they work out sin; and shall I be discontented with this?
What if I have more trouble if I have less sin? The brightest day has its clouds, the purest gold its dross, the most
refined soul some dregs of corruption. The saints lose
nothing in the furnace but what they can well spare, their
dross. Is not this for our good? Why, then, should we
murmur? "I am come to send fire on the earth" (Luke
12:49). Tertullian understands this to be the fire of afflic-

tion. God makes this like the fire of Daniel's three friends, which only burned their bonds and set them at liberty in the furnace. So the fire of affliction serves to burn the bonds of iniquity. "By this therefore shall the iniquity of Jacob be purged; and this is all the fruit, to take away his sin" (Isaiah 27:9). Is there, then, any cause why we should be discontented? God bathes us in the brinish waters of affliction that He may take out our spots. God's people are His husbandry. The plowing of the ground kills the weeds, and the harrowing of the earth breaks the hard clods. God's plowing of us by affliction is to kill the weeds of sin. His harrowing of us is to break the hard clods of impenitence so that the heart may be more fit to receive the seeds of grace; and, if this is His purpose, why should we be discontented?

Afflictions both exercise and increase grace. First, they exercise grace. Affliction breathes our graces. Everything is most excellent when it is most exercised. Our grace, though it cannot be dead, yet may be asleep and needs awakening. What a dull thing the fire is when it is hidden in the embers, or the sun when it is masked by a cloud! A sick man is living, but not lively. Afflictions quicken and excite grace. God does not love to see grace in an eclipse. Now faith puts forth its purest and most noble acts in times of affliction. God makes the fall of the leaf the spring of our graces. So what if we are more passive, if grace is more active?

Second, afflictions increase grace. As the wind serves to increase and blow up the flame, so the windy blasts of affliction augment and blow up our graces. Grace is expended in the furnace, but it is like the widow's oil in the jar, which increased as it was poured out. The torch, when it is beaten, burns the brightest; so does grace when it is exercised by sufferings. Sharp frosts nourish the good corn; so sharp afflictions nourish grace. Some plants grow better in the shade than in the sun, like the bay and the cypress. The shade of adversity is better for some than the sunshine of prosperity. Naturalists observe that cabbage thrives better when it is watered with salt water than with fresh. So some thrive better in the salt water of affliction; and shall we be discontented at that which makes us grow and bear more fruit?

These afflictions bring more of God's immediate presence into the soul. When we are most assaulted, we shall be most assisted. "I will be with thee in trouble" (Psalm 91:15). It cannot be bad with that man whom God, by His gracious presence, is sweetening in the present trial. God will be with us in trouble not only to behold us, but to uphold us—as He was with Daniel in the lions' den and his three friends in the furnace. So what if we have more trouble than others, if we have more of God with us than others have? We never have sweeter smiles from God's face than when the world begins to look strange. "Thy statutes have been my songs" (Psalm 119:54). Where? Not when he was upon the throne, but "in the house of my pilgrimage." We read, "The Lord was not in the wind, not in the earthquake, nor in the fire" (1 Kings 19:11–12); but in a metaphorical and spiritual sense, when the wind of affliction blows upon a believer, God is in the wind. When the fire of affliction kindles upon him, God is in the fire to sanctify, to support, to sweeten. If God is with us, the furnace shall be turned into a festival, the prison into a paradise, the earthquake into a joyful dance. Oh, why should I be discontented when I have more of God's company!

These evils of affliction are for good, as they bring with them certificates of God's love, and are evidences of His special favor. Affliction is the saint's badge and mark of honor. That the God of glory should look upon a worm, and take so much notice of him as to afflict him rather than lose him, is a high act of favor. God's rod is a scepter of dignity. Job calls God's afflicting us His magnifying of us (7:17). Some men's prosperity has been their shame while others' affliction has been their crown.

These afflictions work for our good because they work for us "a far more exceeding weight of glory" (2 Corinthians 4:17). That which works for my glory in heaven works for my good. We do not read in Scripture that any man's honor and riches work for him a weight of glory, but afflictions do; and shall a man be discontented with that which works for his glory? The heavier the weight of affliction, the heavier the weight of glory. Not that our sufferings merit glory, as the Papists wickedly gloss; but though they are not the cause, they are the way. They are not the cause of our crown, yet they are the way to it; and God makes us, as He did our Captain, "perfect through sufferings" (Hebrews 2:10). And shall not all this make us contented with our condition?

Oh, I beseech you, do not look upon the evil of affliction, but the good. Afflictions in Scripture are called "visitations" (Job 7:18). The word in the Hebrew ("to visit") is taken in a good sense as well as a bad one. God's afflictions are but friendly visits. Behold here God's rod like Aaron's rod blossoming, and like Jonathan's rod which had honey at the end of it. Poverty shall starve our sins; the sickness of the body shall cure a sin-sick soul. Oh, then, instead of murmuring and being discontented, bless the Lord. Had you not met with such a rub along the way, you might have gone to hell and never stopped.

ARGUMENT 7. Consider the evil of discontentment. It

has a mixture of grief and danger in it, and both of these must raise a storm in the soul. Have you not seen the posture of a sick man? Sometimes he will sit upon his bed; by and by he will lie down, and when he is down he is not quiet. First he turns on one side and then on the other; he is restless. This is just the emblem of a discontented spirit. The man is not sick, yet he is never well. Sometimes he likes a certain condition of life, and when he has it he is not pleased; he is soon weary, and then he wants another condition of life. This is an evil under the sun. Now the evil of discontent appears in three things:

1. The sordidness of it: it is unworthy of a Christian. First, it is unworthy of his profession. It was the saying of a heathen, "Bear your condition quietly; know you are a man." So I say, bear your condition contentedly; know you are a Christian. You profess to live by faith. What, and are you not content? Faith is a grace that substantiates things not seen. Faith looks beyond the creature and feeds upon promises. Faith does not live by bread alone. When the water in the bottle is spent, faith knows whether to have recourse. Now if a Christian is dejected in the want of visible supplies and recruits, where is faith? "Oh," says one, "my estate in the world is down." Yes, and, what is worse, your faith is down. Will you not be content unless God lets down the vessel to you, as He did to Peter, wherein were all manner of beasts of the earth and fowls of the air (Acts 10:12)? Must you have the first and second course? This is like Thomas, who said, "Unless I put my finger into the print of the nails, I will not believe" (John 20:25). So, unless you have a sensible feeling of outward comforts, you will not be content.

True faith will trust God where it cannot trace Him, and will venture upon God's bond though it has nothing

in view. You who are discontented because you do not
have all you want, let me tell you, either your faith is a
non-entity, or at best it is but an embryo. It is a weak faith
that must have stilts and crutches to support it. No, discontent is not only below faith, but below reason. Why are
you discontented? Is it because you are dispossessed of
such comforts? Well, and do you not have reason to guide
you? Does not reason tell you that you are but tenants at
will? And may not God turn you out when He pleases? You
do not hold your estate by a legal right, but upon favor
and courtesy.

Discontent is unworthy of the relation in which we
stand to God. A Christian is invested with the title and
privilege of sonship (Ephesians 1:5). He is an heir of the
promise. Oh, consider the lot of free grace that has fallen
upon you! You are closely allied to Christ and are of royal
blood. You are advanced, in some sense, above the angels.
"Why then art thou, being the king's son, lean from day to
day?" (2 Samuel 13:4). Why are you discontented? Oh,
how unworthy is this! It is as if the heir to some great
monarch should go pining up and down because he is not
allowed to pick a flower.

2. Consider the sinfulness of it, which appears in three
things: its causes, its concomitants, and its consequences.

It is sinful in its causes, which are these:

Pride. He who thinks highly of his merits usually es-
teems meanly of his condition. A discontented man is a
proud man; he thinks himself better than others, and
therefore finds fault with the wisdom of God that he is not
above others. Thus the thing formed says to Him who
formed it, "Why hast Thou made me thus?" (Romans
9:20). "Why am I not higher?" Discontent is nothing else
but the boiling over of pride.

Envy. Augustine calls envy the sin of the devil. Satan envied Adam's glory in paradise and his robe of innocence. He who envies what his neighbor has is never content with the portion which God's providence parcels out to him. As envy stirs up strife (this made the Plebeian faction so strong among the Romans), so it creates discontent. The envious man looks so much upon the blessings which another enjoys that he cannot see his own mercies, and so continually vexes and tortures himself. Cain envied that his brother's sacrifice was accepted and his own rejected. Hereupon he was discontented, and presently murderous thoughts began to arise in his heart.

Covetousness. This is a radical sin. Whence are vexing lawsuits but from discontent? And whence is discontent but from covetousness? Covetousness and contentedness cannot dwell in the same heart. Avarice is a hell that is never satisfied. A covetous man is like the behemoth: "Behold he drinketh up a river, he trusteth that he can draw up Jordan into his mouth" (Job 40:23). There are four things, Solomon said, that say, "It is not enough" (Proverbs 30:15–16). I may add a fifth, the heart of a covetous man; he is still craving. Covetousness is like a wolf in the breast which is ever feeding, and, because a man is not satisfied, he is never content.

Jealousy. This is sometimes occasioned through melancholy and sometimes through misapprehension. The spirit of jealousy causes this evil spirit. Jealousy is the rage of man (Proverbs 6:34); and often this is nothing but suspicion and fancy, yet such as creates real discontent.

Distrust. This reflectss a great degree of atheism. The discontented person is ever distrustful. "The bill of provision grows low. I am in these straits and exigencies, and can God help me? Can He prepare a table in the wilderness? Surely He cannot! My estate is exhausted; can God restore me? My friends are gone; can God raise up more? Surely the arm of His power is shrunk. I am like the dry fleece; can any water come upon this fleece? 'If the Lord would make windows in heaven, might this thing be?' (2 Kings 7:2)." Thus, the anchor of hope and the shield of faith being cast away, the soul goes pining up and down.

Discontent is nothing else but the echo of unbelief, and, remember, distrust is worse than distress.

Discontent is evil in its concomitants, which are two:

(1) Discontent is joined with a sullen melancholy. A Christian of right temper should be ever cheerful in God. "Serve the Lord with gladness" (Psalm 100:2). It is a sign that the oil of grace has been poured into the heart when the oil of gladness shines in the countenance. Cheerfulness credits religion. How can the discontented person be cheerful? Discontent is a dogged, sullen humor. Because we do not have what we desire, God shall not have a good word or look from us. It is as with a bird in the cage: because she is pent up and cannot fly in the open air, therefore she beats herself against the cage and is ready to kill herself. Thus said that peevish prophet in Jonah 4:9: "I do well to be angry even unto death."

(2) Discontent is accompanied by unthankfulness. Because we do not have all that we desire, we do not mind the mercies which we have. We deal with God as the widow of Zarephath did with the prophet. The prophet Elijah had been a means to keep her alive in the famine, for it was for her sake that her meal in the barrel and her oil in the jar failed not. But as soon as her son died, she fell into a passion and began to quarrel with the prophet: "What have I to do with thee, O thou man of God? Art thou come to call my sin to remembrance, and to slay my

son?" (1 Kings 17:18).

This is how ungratefully we deal with God. We can be content to receive mercies from God, but if He crosses us in the least thing, then, through discontent, we grow irritable and impatient, ready to fly upon God. Thus God loses all His mercies. We read in Scripture of the thank offering; the discontented person cuts God short of this, and the Lord loses His thank offering. A discontented Christian repines in the midst of mercies as did Adam, who sinned in the midst of paradise. Discontent is a spider that sucks the poison of unthankfulness out of the sweetest flower of God's blessings, and by a devilish chemistry extracts dross out of the most refined gold. The discontented person thinks everything he does for God is too much, and everything God does for him is too little.

Oh, what a sin is unthankfulness! It is an accumulative sin. What Cicero said of parricide, I may say of ingratitude: "There are many sins bound up in this one sin." It is a voluminous wickedness, and how full of sin is discontent! A discontented Christian, because he does not have all the world, therefore dishonors God with the mercies that he has. God made Eve out of Adam's rib to be a helper (as Chrysostom says), but the devil made an arrow of this rib and shot Adam in the heart. So discontent takes the rib of God's mercy and ungratefully shoots at Him. Estate and liberty shall be employed against God. Thus it is oftentimes. Behold, then, how discontent and ingratitude are interwoven and twisted one within another. Thus discontent is sinful in its concomitants.

Finally, discontent is sinful in its consequences. First, it makes a man very unlike the Spirit of God. The Spirit of God is a meek Spirit. The Holy Ghost descended in the likeness of a dove (Matthew 3:16). A dove is the emblem of meekness. A discontented spirit is not a meek spirit. It makes a man like the devil. The devil, being swelled with the poison of envy and malice, is never content. Just so are the discontented. The devil is an unquiet spirit; he is still walking about (1 Peter 5:8). It is his rest to be walking. And herein is the discontented person like him, for he goes up and down, vexing himself, seeking rest and finding none. He is the picture of the devil.

Discontent disjoins the soul; it untunes the heart for duty. "Is any man afflicted? Let him pray" (James 5:13). But is any man discontented? How shall he pray? "Lift up pure hands without wrath" (1 Timothy 2:8). Discontent is full of wrath and passion. The malcontent cannot lift up pure hands; he lifts up leprous hands. He poisons his prayers. Will God accept a poisoned sacrifice? Chrysostom compares prayer to a fine garland. Those who make a garland, he said, must have clean hands. Prayer is a precious garland; the heart that makes it needs to be clean. Discontent throws poison into the spring. Discontent puts the heart into a disorder and mutiny, and one cannot serve the Lord without distraction.

Discontent sometimes unfits for the very use of reason. Jonah, in a passion of discontent, spoke no better than blasphemy and nonsense. "I do well to be angry even unto death," he said in Jonah 4:9. What? To be angry with God? To die for anger? Surely he did not know what he said. When discontent transports us, then, like Moses, we speak unadvisedly with our lips. This humor even suspends the very acts of reason.

Discontent not only disquiets a man's self, but those who are near him. This evil spirit troubles families, parishes, and the like. If there is only one string out of tune, it spoils all the music. One discontented spirit makes

jarrings and discords among others. It is this ill humor
that breeds quarrels and lawsuits. Whence is all our contention but for want of contentment? From whence "come
wars and fightings among you? Come they not hence,
even of your lusts?" (James 4:1)—in particular, from this
lust of discontent. Why did Absalom start a war against his
father, and why would he have taken off not only his
crown, but his head as well? Was it not his discontent?
Absalom would be king. Why did Ahab stone Naboth? Was
he not discontent about the vineyard? Oh, this devil of
discontent! Thus you have seen the sinfulness of it.

Consider also the folly of discontent. I may say with the
psalmist, "Surely they are disquieted in vain" (Psalm 39:6).
Is it not a vain, simple thing to be troubled at the loss of
that which is, in its own nature, perishing and change-
able? God has filled the world with change, and for me to
meet with inconstancy here, to lose a friend or estate, to
be in a constant fluctuation, is no more than to see a
flower wither or a leaf drop off in autumn. There is an autumn upon every comfort, a fall of the leaf. Now it is extreme folly to be discontented at the loss of those things
which are, in their own nature, perishable. What Solomon
said of riches is true of all things under the sun: "they take
wings." Noah's dove brought an olive branch in its mouth,
but presently flew out of the ark and never returned
again. Such a comfort brings honey to us in its mouth, but
it has wings. And to what purpose should we be troubled
unless we had wings to fly after and overtake it?

Discontent is heart-breaking; it takes away the comfort
of life. "By sorrow of the heart the spirit is broken"
(Proverbs 15:13). There is not one of us who does not
have many mercies if we could just see them. But, because
we do not have all that we desire, we lose the comfort of

that which we have. Jonah, having his gourd smitten (a withering vanity), was so discontented that he never thought of his miraculous deliverance out of the whale's belly. He took no comfort from his life, but wished that he might die. What folly is this? We must have all or none. In this we are like children who throw away the piece which is cut for them because it is not bigger. Discontent eats out the comfort of life.

Besides, it would be well if we seriously weighed how prejudicial this is even to our health. For as discontent distresses the mind, so it pines the body. It frets like a moth and, by wasting the spirits, weakens the vitals. The pleurisy of discontent brings the body into a consumption; and is this not folly?

Discontent does not ease our burden, but makes the cross heavier. A contented spirit goes cheerfully under its affliction. Discontent makes our grief as unbearable as it is unreasonable. If the leg is well, it can endure a fetter and not complain; but if the leg is sore, then the fetters are troubling. Discontent of mind is the sore that makes the fetters of affliction more grievous. Discontent troubles us more than the trouble itself; it steeps the affliction in wormwood. When Christ was upon the cross, the Jews brought him gall and vinegar to drink that it might add to His sorrow. Discontent brings to a man in affliction gall and vinegar to drink; this is worse than the affliction itself. Is it not folly for a man to embitter his own cross?

Discontent spins out our troubles longer. A Christian is discontented because he is in want, and therefore he is in want because he is discontented. He murmurs because he is afflicted, and therefore he is afflicted because he murmurs. Discontent delays and sets aside our mercies. God deals with us here as we used to do with our children.

When they are quiet and cheerful, they shall have anything; but if we see them cry and fret, then we withhold from them. We get nothing from God by our discontent but blows. The more the child struggles, the more it is beaten. When we struggle with God by our sinful passions, He doubles and triples His strokes.

God will tame our cursed hearts. What did Israel get by their peevishness? They were within eleven days' journey of Canaan. And then they were discontented and began to murmur, so God led them on a march forty years long in the wilderness. Is it not folly for us to cut off our own mercies? Thus you have seen the evil of discontent.

ARGUMENT 8. The next argument or motive to contentment is this: why is a man not content with the competence which he has? Perhaps if he had more, he would be less content. Covetousness is a dry drunkenness. The world is such that the more we have, the more we crave. It cannot fill the heart of man. When the fire burns, how do you quench it? Not by pouring oil on the flame or by laying on more wood, but by withdrawing the fuel. When the appetite is enflamed after riches, how may a man be satisfied? Not by having just what he desires, but by withdrawing the fuel, that is, by moderating and lessening his desires. He who is contented has enough. A man in a fever or a dropsy thirsts. How do you satisfy him? Not by giving him liquid things which will enflame his thirst all the more, but by removing the cause, and so curing his distemper. The way for a man to be contented is not by raising his estate higher, but by bringing his heart lower.

ARGUMENT 9. The next argument to contentment is the shortness of life. It is but a vapor (James 4:14). Life is a wheel ever running. The poets painted time with wings to show the volubility and swiftness of it. Job compares it to a swift runner (Job 9:25), and to a day, not a year. It is indeed like a day. Infancy is, as it were, the daybreak; youth is the sunrise; full growth is the sun in the meridian; old age is sunset; sickness is the evening; then comes the night of death. How quickly is this day of life spent! Oftentimes this sun goes down at noon; life ends before the evening of old age comes. Nay, sometimes the sun of life sets presently after sunrise. Quickly after the dawning of infancy, the night of death approaches. Oh, how short is the life of man! The consideration of the brevity of life may spur the heart to contentment.

Remember, you are to be here but a day. You have but a short way to go; and what need is there for long provision for a short way? If a traveler has but enough to bring him to his journey's end, he desires no more. We have but a day to live, and perhaps we may be in the twelfth hour of the day. Why, if God gives us but enough to bear our charges until night, it is sufficient; let us be content. If a man had the lease of a house or farm but for two or three days, and should fall to building and planting, would he not be judged as very indiscreet? So, when we have but a short time here, and death calls us presently off the stage, is it not extreme folly to thirst immoderately after the world and pull down our souls to build up an estate? Therefore, as Esau said once in a profane sense concerning his birthright, "Lo, I am at the point of dying, and what profit shall this birthright do to me?" So, let a Christian say, in a religious sense, "Lo, I am even at the point of death; my grave is going to be made, and what good will the world do me? If I have but enough until sunset, I am content."

ARGUMENT 10. Consider seriously the nature of a prosperous condition in these three things:

1. More trouble. Many who have an abundance of all things to enjoy do not have as much contentment and sweetness in their lives as some who must do hard labor. Sad, solicitous thoughts often attend a prosperous condition. Care is the evil spirit which haunts the rich man and will not suffer him to be quiet. When his chests are full of gold, his heart is full of care, either how to manage, how to increase, or how to secure what he has gotten. Oh, the troubles and perplexities that wait upon prosperity! The world's high seats are very uneasy. Sunshine is pleasant, but sometimes it scorches with its heat. The bee gives honey, but sometimes it stings. Prosperity has its sweetness and its sting. Competence with contentment is far more desirable. Never did Jacob sleep better than when he had the heavens for his canopy and a hard stone for his pillow. A large, voluminous estate is but like a long, trailing garment which is more troublesome than useful.

2. In a prosperous condition there is more danger, and that in two ways:

First, in respect of a man's self. The rich man's table is often his snare. He is ready to engulf himself too deep in these sweet waters. In this sense, it is hard to know how to abound. It must be a strong brain that bears heady wine. He must have much wisdom and grace who knows how to bear a high condition. Either he is ready to kill himself with care or surfet himself upon delicious delights. Oh, the hazard of honor, the damage of dignity! Pride, security, and rebellion are the worms that are bred by plenty. The pastures of prosperity are rank and surfetting. How soon are we broken upon the soft pillow of ease? Prosperity is often a trumpet that sounds a retreat; it calls men off from the pursuit of religion. The sun of prosperity often dulls and puts out the fire of zeal. How many souls has the pleurisy of abundance killed? They who will be rich fall into snares. The world is bird-lime at our feet; it is full of golden sands, but they are quicksands. Prosperity, like smooth Jacob, will supplant and betray. A great estate without much vigilance will be a thief to rob us of heaven. Such as are in the pinnacle of honor are in the most danger of falling.

A lower estate is less hazardous. The little sailing ship rides safe by the shore when the gallant ship, advancing with its mast and topsail, is cast away. Adam in paradise was overcome, while Job on the dunghill was a conqueror. Samson fell asleep on Delilah's lap; some have fallen so fast asleep on the lap of ease and plenty that they have never awakened until they have been in hell. The world's fawning is worse than its frowning, and it is more to be feared when it smiles than when it thunders. Prosperity in Scripture is compared to a candle. Job 29:3: "When His candle shined upon my head." How many have burned their wings upon this candle!

The corn, being overripe, sheds; and fruit, when it mellows, begins to rot. When men mellow with the sun of prosperity, commonly their souls begin to rot in sin. "How hard is it for a rich man to enter into the kingdom of heaven!" (Luke 18:24). His golden weights keep him from ascending up the hill of God; and shall we not be content though we are placed in a lower orb? What if we are not in as much bravery and gallantry as others? We are not in as much danger. As we lack the honor of the world, so the temptations. Oh, the abundance of danger that is in abundance! We see by common experience that lunatics, when the moon is declining and in the wane, are sober enough; but when it is a full moon, they are more wild and exorbitant. When men's estates are waning, they are more serious about their souls, more humble; but when it is the full of the moon and they have an abundance, then their hearts begin to swell with their estates and are scarcely themselves.

Those who write concerning the various climates observe that such as live in the northern parts of the world, if you bring them into the southern part, lose their stomachs and die quickly; but if those who live in the more southern, hot climates come into the north, their stomachs mend and they live long. Give me leave to apply this. Bring a man from the cold, starving climate of poverty into the hot, southern climate of prosperity and he begins to lose his appetite for good things. He grows weak, and the chances are a thousand to one that all his religion will not die. But bring a Christian from the south to the north, from a rich, nourishing estate into a dull, low condition— let him come into a colder and hungrier air—and then his stomach mends; he has a better appetite after heavenly things. He hungers more after Christ; he thirsts more for grace; he eats more at one meal of the bread of life than at six before. This man is now likely to live and hold out in his religion. Be content, then, with a little. If you have but enough to pay for your passage to heaven, it suffices.

Second, a prosperous condition is dangerous in regard to others. A great estate, for the most part, draws envy to it. David, as a shepherd, was quiet; but David, the courtier, was pursued by his enemies. An envious man does not know how to live except upon the ruin of his neighbor. He raises himself higher by bringing others lower. Prosperity is an eyesore to many. The sheep that have the most wool are soonest fleeced. The barren tree grows peaceably. No man meddles with the ash or the willow, but the apple tree shall have many rude suitors. Oh, then, be content to carry a lesser sail! He who has lesser revenues has less envy. Such as bear the fairest frontispiece, and make the greatest show in the world, are the target for envy and malice to shoot at.

3. A prosperous condition has a greater reckoning in it. Every man must be responsible for his talents. You who have great possessions in the world, do you use your estate for God's glory? Are you rich in good works? Grace makes a private person a common good. Do you disburse your money for public uses? It is lawful, in this sense, to put out our money to use. Oh, let us all remember that an estate is a deposit! We are but stewards, and our Lord and Master will before long say, "Give an account of your stewardship." The greater our estate, the greater our charge. The more our revenues, the more our reckonings. You who have less in this world, be content. God will expect less from you where He has sowed more sparingly.

ARGUMENT 11. Consider the example of those who have been eminent in contentment. Examples are usually more forcible than precepts. Abraham, being called out to hot service, and one who was against flesh and blood, was content. God bade him offer up his son, Isaac. This was great work. Isaac was the son of his old age, the son of his love, the son of the promise. Christ, the Messiah, was to come of his line. "In Isaac shall thy seed be blessed" (Genesis 22:18). So that to offer up Isaac seemed not only to oppose Abraham's reason, but his faith, too; for if Isaac were to die, the world (for all he knew) must be without a Mediator. Besides, if Isaac was sacrificed, was there no other hand to do it but Abraham's? Must the father be the executioner? Must he who was the instrument of giving Isaac his being be the instrument of taking it away? Yet Abraham did not dispute or hesitate, but believed against hope and was content with God's prescription. So, when God called him to leave his country, he was content. Some would have argued thus: "What? Leave all my friends, my native soil, my brave situation, and go turn pilgrim?" Abraham was content. Besides, Abraham went blind-folded: "He knew not where he went" (Hebrews 11:8). God held him in suspense; he must go wandering he knew not where. And when he came to the place God had laid out for him, he did not know what opposition he would meet with there. The world seldom casts a favorable aspect upon strangers, yet he was content and obeyed. He sojourned in the land of promise.

Behold briefly his pilgrimage. First, he went to Haran, a city in Mesopotamia. When he had sojourned there for awhile, his father died. Then he moved to Shechem, then to Bethlehem in Canaan. There a famine arose. Then he went down to Egypt. After that he returned to Canaan. When he came there, he came with a promise, but he found nothing to answer his expectation. He did not have one foot of land, but was an exile. In this time of his sojourning, he buried his wife, and as for his dwellings, he had no sumptuous buildings, but led his life in poor cottages. All this was enough to have broken any man's heart. Abraham might have thought thus to himself: "Is this the land I must possess? Here is no probability of anything good; all things are against me." Well, was he discontented? No, for God had said to him, "Abraham, go, leave your country," and this word was enough to lead him all the world over. He was presently upon his march. Here was a man who had learned to be content.

But let us descend a little lower to heathen Zeno, of whom Seneca speaks, who had once been very rich. Hearing of a shipwreck, and that all his goods were drowned at sea, he said, "Fortune has dwelt well with me, and would now have me study philosophy." He was content to change his course of life, to leave off being a merchant and to turn philosopher. And if a heathen said this, shall not a Christian much more say when the world is drained from him, "God would have me leave off following the world and study Christ more, and how to get to heaven"!

Do I see a heathen contented and a Christian disquieted? How do heathens vilify those things which Christians magnify? Though they did not know God, or what true happiness meant, yet they would speak very highly of a deity, and of the life to come, as did Aristotle and Plato; and in favor of those Elysian delights which they only fancied, they undervalued and condemned the things here below. It was the doctrine they taught their scholars, and which some of them practiced, that men should strive to be contented with a little. They were willing to make an exchange, to have less gold and more learning; and shall we not be content, then, to have less of the world so we may have more of Christ? May not Christians blush to see heathens content with minimal sustenance, as much as would replenish nature, and to see themselves so transported with the love of earthly things? If their possessions begin to abate a little, and the bill of provision grows short, they murmur and say like Micah, "Have ye taken away my gods, and do you ask me what I ail?" (Judges 18:24). Have heathens gone this far in contentment? Is it not sad for us to fall short of those who come short of heaven?

These heroes of their time, how did they embrace death itself? Socrates died in prison; Hercules was burned alive; Cato (whom Seneca calls the lively image and portrait of virtue) was thrust through with a sword; but how bravely, and with what contentment of spirit did they die! "Shall I," said Seneca, "weep for Cato, or Regulus, or the rest of those worthies who died with so much valor and patience?" Did not cross providences make them to alter their countenance, and do I see a Christian appalled and amazed? Did death not frighten them, and does it distract us? Did the springhead of nature rise so high, and shall not grace, like the waters of the sanctuary, rise higher? We who pretend to live by faith, may we not go to school under those who had no other pilot but reason to guide them?

No, let me come a step lower, to creatures devoid of reason. We see that every creature is content with its allowance—the beasts with their food, the birds with their nests. They live only upon providence; and shall we make ourselves below them? Let a Christian go to the school of the ox and the ass and learn contentment. We think we never have enough and are still laying up. The fowls of the air do not lay up: "they reap not, nor gather into barns" (Matthew 6:26). It is an argument which Christ brings to make Christians contented with their condition. The birds do not lay up, yet they are provided for and are contented. "Are ye not much better than they?" said Christ. But if you are discontented, are you not much worse than they? Let these examples quicken us.

ARGUMENT 12. Whatever change or trouble a child of God meets with, it is all the hell he shall have. Whatever eclipse may be upon his name or estate, I may say of it, as Athanasius said of his banishment, that it is a little cloud which will soon blow over; and then his gulf is crossed, his hell is past.

Death begins a wicked man's hell, but it puts an end to a godly man's hell. Think to yourself, "What if I endure

this? It is but a temporary hell." Indeed, if all our hell is
here, it is but an easy hell. What is the cup of affliction
compared to the cup of damnation? Lazarus could not get
a crumb. He was so diseased that the dogs took pity on
him and, as if they had been his physicians, licked his
sores; but this was an easy hell. The angels quickly fetched
him out of it. If all our hell is in this life, in the midst of
this hell we may have the love of God—and then it is no
longer hell, but paradise. If our hell is here, we may see to
the bottom of it; it is but skin-deep and cannot touch the
soul. And we may see to the end of it. It is a hell that is
short-lived. After a wet night of affliction comes a bright
morning of the resurrection. If our lives are short, our trials cannot be long. As our riches take wings and fly, so do
our sufferings. Then let us be content.

ARGUMENT 13. Finally, to have sufficient means for
the necessities of life, to have a competency and yet lack
contentment, is a great judgment. If a man has a huge
stomach so that, whatever meat you give him, he is still
craving more and never satisfied, you would say this is a
great judgment upon the man. You who are a devourer of
money, and yet never have enough but cry, "Give, give,"
this is your judgment: "They shall eat and not have
enough" (Hosea 4:10). As the throat of a malicious man is
an open sepulchre, so is the heart of a covetous man.
Covetousness is not only a sin, but the punishment of a
sin. It is a secret curse upon a covetous person that he
shall thirst and thirst and never be satisfied. "He that
loveth silver shall not be satisfied with silver" (Ecclesiastes
5:10). And is this not a curse?

What was it but a severe judgment upon the people of
Judah? "Ye eat, but ye have not enough; ye drink, but ye
are not filled with drink" (Haggai 1:6). Oh, let us take

heed of this plague! Did Esau say to his brother, "I have abundance, my brother" (Genesis 33:9), or, as we translate it, "I have enough"? And shall not a Christian say so much more? It is sad that our hearts should be so dead to heavenly things, and like a sponge to suck in earthly things. Let all that has been said work our minds to holy contentment.

Chapter 12

Three Necessary Cautions

Next, I will lay down some necessary cautions. Though I say a man should be content in every state, yet there are three states in which he must not be content.

1. He must not be contented in a natural state. Here he must learn not to be content. A sinner in his pure natural state is under the wrath of God (John 3:36); and shall he be content when that dreadful vial is going to be poured out? Is it nothing to be under the scorchings of divine fury? Who can dwell with everlasting burnings? A sinner as a sinner is "under the power of Satan" (Acts 26:18); and shall he, in this state, be content? Who would be content to stay in the enemy's quarters? While we sleep in the lap of sin, the devil does to us as the Philistines did to Samson: he cuts the lock of our strength and puts out our eyes. Be not content, O sinner, in this state. If a man is in debt, body and soul, in fear every hour that he will be arrested and carried as a prisoner to hell—shall he now be content? Here I preach against contentment. Oh, get out of this condition!

I would hasten you out of it as the angel hastened Lot out of Sodom. There is the smell of fire and brimstone upon you. The longer a man stays in his sin, the more sin is strengthened. It is hard to get out of sin when the heart, like a garrison, is fed and fortified. A young plant is easily removed, but when the tree is once rooted there is no stirring it. You who are rooted in your pride, unbelief, and

impenitence, it will cost you many a sad pull before you
are plucked out of your natural state. It is a hard thing to
have a brazen face and a broken heart. "He travaileth with
iniquity" (Psalm 7:14). Be assured that the longer you
travel with your sins, the more and the sharper pangs you
must expect in the new birth. Oh, do not be content with
your natural condition!

David said, "Why art thou disquieted, O my soul?"
(Psalm 43:5), but a sinner should say to himself, "Why are
you *not* disquieted, O my soul?" Why is it that you lay afflictions so to heart and cannot lay sin to heart? It is a
mercy when we are disquieted about sin. It is better for a
man to be troubled at the setting of a bone than to be
lame and in pain all his life. Blessed is that trouble which
brings the soul to Christ. It is one of the worst sights to see
a bad conscience quiet. Of the two, a fever is better than a
lethargy. I wonder to see a man in his natural state be content. What, content to go to hell?

2. Though in regard to external things a man should
be content in every state, yet he must not be content in
such a conditon wherein God is apparently dishonored. If
a man's trade is such that he can hardly use it without tres-
passing upon a command (and so making a trade of sin),
he must not content himself in such a condition. God
never called any man to such a calling as is sinful. A man
in this case had better knock off and divert his efforts
elsewhere. Better to lose some of his gain so he may lessen
some of his guilt. So for servants who live in a profane
family (the suburb of hell), where the name of God is not
called upon unless it is taken in vain, they are not to content themselves in such a place. They are to come out of
the tents of these sinners. There is a double danger in living among the profane:

(1) Lest we come to be infected with the poison of their example. Joseph, living in Pharaoh's court, had learned to swear by the life of Pharaoh (Genesis 42:15). We are prone to such by example. Men take in deeper impressions by the eye than by the ear. Dives was a bad pattern, and he had many brethren who, seeing him sin, trod precisely in the same steps. Therefore he said, "I pray thee, send him to my father's house, for I have five brethren, that he may testify to them, that they come not to this place of torment" (Luke 16:27–28). Dives knew which way they went.

It is easy to catch a disease from another, but not to catch health. The bad will sooner corrupt the good than the good will convert the bad. Take an equal quantity and proportion, so much sweet wine with so much sour vinegar; the vinegar will sooner sour the wine than the wine will sweeten the vinegar. Sin is compared to the plague (I Kings 8:38) and to leaven (1 Corinthians 5:7) to show of what a spreading nature it is. A bad master makes a bad servant. Jacob's cattle, by looking on the rods which were speckled, conceived like the rods. We do as we see others do before us, and especially above us. If the head is sick, the other parts of the body are distempered. If the sun does not shine upon the mountains, it must set in the valleys. We pray, "Lead us not into temptation," and do we lead ourselves into temptation? Lot was the world's miracle, in that he kept himself fresh in Sodom's salt water.

(2) By living in an evil family, we are liable to incur their punishment: "Pour out Thy wrath upon the families that call not upon Thy name" (Jeremiah 13:25). For want of pouring out prayers, the wrath of God was ready to be poured out. It is dangerous living in the tents of Kedar. When God sends His flying scroll, written within and with-

out with curses, it enters "into the house of the thief and perjurer, and it consumes the timber and the stones thereof" (Zechariah 5:4). Is it not of sad consequence to live in a profane, perjured family, when the sin of the governor pulls his house down around his ears? If the stone and timber are destroyed, how shall the servants escape? Suppose God does not send a temporal scroll of curses in the family; there is a spiritual scroll, and that is worse!

Do not be content to live where religion dies. "Salute the brethren, and Nymphas, and the church which is in his house" (Colossians 4:15). The house of the godly is a little church, the house of the wicked a little hell. Oh, incorporate yourselves into a religious family; the house of a good man is perfumed with a blessing. When the holy oil of grace is poured upon the head, the savor of this ointment sweetly diffuses itself, and the virtue of it runs down upon the skirts of the family. Pious examples are very magnetic and powerful. Seneca said to his sister, "Though I leave you not wealth, yet I will leave you a good example." Let us engraft ourselves among the saints. By being often among the spices, we come to smell like them.

3. The third caution is that, though in every condition we must be content, yet we are not to content ourselves with a little grace. Grace is the best blessing. Though we should be content with an adequacy of estate, yet not with an adequacy of grace. It was the end of Christ's ascension to heaven to give gifts, and the end of those gifts is "that we may grow up into Him who is the Head, Christ" (Ephesians 4:15). Where the apostle distinguishes between our being in Christ and our growing in Him—our engrafting and our flourishing—do not be content with a modicum in religion.

It is not enough that there is life, but there must be

fruit. Barrenness under the law was accounted a curse. The farther we are from fruit, the nearer we are to cursing. It is a sad thing when men are fruitful only in the unfruitful works of darkness. Be not content with a dram or two of grace. Next to a stillborn, a starveling in Christ is worst. Oh, covet more grace. Never think you have enough. It is good and honest avarice. We are bidden to covet the best things (1 Corinthians 12:31). It is a heavenly ambition when we desire to be high in God's favor, a blessed contention when all the strife is over who shall be most holy.

St. Paul, though he was content with a little of the world, was not content with a little grace. He "reached forward, and pressed towards the mark of the high calling of God in Christ Jesus" (Philippians 3:13–14). A true Christian is a wonder. He is the most contented, yet the least satisfied. He is contented with a morsel of bread and a little water in the jar, yet never satisfied with grace. He pants and breathes after more. This is his prayer: "Lord, more conformity to Christ, more communion with Christ." He would fain have Christ's image pictured in a more lively way upon his soul. True grace is always progressive. As the saints are called lamps and stars in regard to their light, so they are called trees of righteousness for their growth (Isaiah 61:3). They are indeed like the tree of life, bringing forth several sorts of fruit.

A true Christian grows in beauty. Grace is the best complexion of the soul. It is, at the first planting, like Rachel: fair to look upon, but, the more it lives, the more it sends forth its rays of beauty. Abraham's faith was beautiful at first, but at last it shone in its orient colors and grew so illustrious that God Himself was in love with it, and made his faith a pattern to all believers.

A true Christian grows in sweetness. A poisonous weed may grow as much as the hyssop or rosemary, the poppy in the field like the corn; the crabapple as the pear, but the one has a harsh, sour taste, while the other mellows as it grows. A hypocrite may grow in outward dimensions as much as a child of God. He may pray as much and profess as much, but he grows only in magnitude; he brings forth sour grapes, and his duties are leaven with pride. The true believer ripens as he grows. He grows in love, humility, and faith, which mellow and sweeten his duties, and make them come off with a better relish. The believer grows as the flower; he casts a fragrancy and perfume.

A true Christian grows in strength. He grows still more rooted and settled. The more the tree grows, the more it spreads its root in the earth. For a Christian, who is a plant of the heavenly Jerusalem, the longer he grows, the more he incorporates into Christ and sucks spiritual juice and sap from Him. He is a dwarf in regard to humility, but a giant in regard to strength. He is strong to do duties, to bear burdens, to resist temptations.

He grows in the exercise of his grace. He not only has oil in his lamps, but his lamps are burning and shining. Grace is agile and dexterous. Christ's vines flourish, and hence we read of a lively hope (1 Peter 1:3) and a fervent love (1 Peter 1:22). Here is the activity of grace. Indeed, sometimes grace is as a sleepy habit in the soul, like sap in the vine—not exerting its vigor, due to spiritual sloth or by reason of falling into some sin—but this is only for a while. The spring of grace will come, the flowers will appear, and the fig tree will put forth her green figs. The fresh gales of the Spirit sweetly revive grace. The Church of Christ, whose heart was a garden and her graces as precious spices, prays for the heavenly breathings of the

Spirit, that her sacred spices might flow out.

A true Christian grows both in the kind and in the degree of grace. In his spiritual living, he gets an augmentation. He adds to faith virtue; to virtue knowledge; to knowledge temperance, and so on. Here is grace growing, in its kind, and he goes on from faith to faith (Romans 1:17). There is also grace growing in its degree. "We are bound to give thanks to God for you, brethren, because your faith groweth exceedingly" (2 Thessalonians 1:3). It increases over and above. And the Apostle speaks of those spiritual plants which were laden with gospel fruit (Philippians 1:11). A Christian is compared to the vine, an emblem of fruitfulness. He must bear full clusters. We are bidden to perfect that which is lacking in our faith (1 Thessalonians 3:10). A Christian must never be so old as to be past bearing. He brings forth fruit in his old age (Psalm 92:14). A heaven-born plant is ever growing. He never thinks he grows enough. He is not content unless he adds one cubit every day to his spiritual stature.

We must not be content just with so much grace as will keep life and soul together. A dram or two must not suffice, but we must still be increasing with the increase of God (Colossians 2:19). We need to renew our strength as the eagle. Our sins are renewed, our wants are renewed, our temptations are renewed, and shall not our strength be renewed? Oh, be not content with the first embryo of grace, grace in its infancy and youth. Do you look for degrees of glory? Then be Christians of degrees. Though a believer should be content with a modest estate, yet not with a modicum in religion. A Christian of the right breed labors still to perfect himself, and come nearer unto that holiness in God, Who is the original, the pattern and prototype of all holiness.

Chapter 13

How a Christian May Know Whether
He Has Learned This Divine Art

USE OF TRIAL. Having laid down these three cautions, I proceed in the next place to a use of trial. How may a Christian know that he has learned this lesson of contentment? I shall lay down some characteristics by which you shall know it.

1. A contented spirit is a silent spirit. He does not have one word to say against God. "I was dumb (or silent) because Thou, Lord, didst it" (Psalm 39:9). Contentment silences all dispute. "He sitteth alone and keepeth silence" (Lamentations 3:28). There is a sinful silence when God is dishonored, His truth wounded, and men hold their peace. This silence is a loud sin. And there is a holy silence, when the soul sits down quiet and content with its condition. When Samuel told Eli that heavy message from God, that He would "judge his house, and that the iniquity of his family should not be purged away with sacrifice forever" (1 Samuel 3:13), did Eli murmur or dispute? No, he did not have one word to say against God. "It is the Lord; let Him do what seemeth Him good" (verse 18).

A discontented spirit says, as did Pharaoh, "Who is the Lord? Why should I suffer all this? Why should I be brought into this low condition? Who is the Lord?" But a gracious heart says, as did Eli, "It is the Lord; let Him do what He will with me." When Nadab and Abihu, the sons

106

of Aaron, had offered up strange fire, and fire went from the Lord and devoured them (Leviticus 10:1–2), was Aaron in a passion of discontent? No, "Aaron held his peace." A contented spirit is never angry unless it is with himself for having hard thoughts of God. When Jonah said, "I do well to be angry," this was not a contented spirit; it was not becoming a prophet.

2. A contented spirit is a cheerful spirit. The Greeks call it *euthumeo,* a good spirit. Contentment is something more than patience, for patience only denotes submission. Contentment denotes cheerfulness. A contented Christian is more than passive. He does not only bear the cross, but he takes up the cross. He looks upon God as a wise God, and on whatever He does as in order to achieve a cure. Hence the contented Christian is cheerful and "takes pleasure in infirmities and distresses" as the apostle says in 2 Corinthians 12:10). He not only submits to God's dealings, but rejoices in them. He not only says "the Lord is just in all that has befallen me," but "the Lord is good." This is to be content.

A sullen melancholy is hateful. It is said, "God loves a cheerful giver" (2 Corinthians 9:7). Aye, and God loves a cheerful liver. We are bidden in Scripture not to be careful, but we are nowhere bidden not to be cheerful. He who is contented with his condition does not lose his spiritual joy; and indeed he has that within him which is the ground of cheerfulness. He carries a pardon sealed within his heart.

3. A contented spirit is a thankful spirit. This is a degree above the other. "In everything give thanks" (1 Thessalonians 5:18). A gracious heart spies mercy in every condition; therefore he has his heart lifted up to thankfulness. Others will bless God for prosperity, but he blesses

Him for affliction. Thus he reasons with himself: "Am I in want? God sees it as better for me to want than to abound. God is now dieting me. He sees it as better for my spiritual health sometimes to be fasting." Therefore, he not only submits, but is thankful. The malcontent is ever complaining of his condition; the contented spirit is ever giving thanks. Oh, what height of grace is this! A contented heart is a temple where the praises of God are sung forth, not a sepulchre wherein they are buried. A contented Christian, in the greatest straits, has his heart enlarged and dilated in thankfulness. He often contemplates God's love in election. He sees that he is a monument of mercy; therefore he desires to be a pattern of praise. There is always congratulatory music in a contented soul; the spirit of grace works in the heart like new wine which, under the heaviest pressures of sorrows, will have a vent open for thankfulness. This is to be content.

4. When a person is content, no condition comes amiss to him. So it is in this text: "in whatsoever state I am." A contented Christian can accept anything, whether want or abundance. The people of Israel knew neither how to abound nor how to want. When they were in want they murmured, "Can God prepare a table in the wilderness?" And when they ate and were filled, then they lifted up the heel.

Paul knew how to manage every estate: he could be either a note higher or a note lower. He was, in this sense, a universalist: he could do anything that God would have him do. If he were in prosperity, he knew how to be thankful; he was neither lifted up with the one nor cast down with the other; he could carry a greater sail or a lesser one.

Thus a contented Christian knows how to come to

terms with any condition. There are some who can be content in some state, but not in every state. They can be content in a wealthy state, when they have the streams of milk and honey; while God's candle shines upon their head they are content. But if the wind turns and is against them they are discontented. While they have a silver crutch to lean upon they are content; but if God breaks this crutch, they are discontented.

But Paul had learned in every state to carry himself with equanimity of mind. Others could be content with their affliction if God would give them leave to pick and choose. They could be content to bear such a cross; they could better endure sickness than poverty, better endure loss of estate than loss of children. If they might have another man's cross, they could be content; any condition but the present one—this is not to be content.

A contented Christian does not seek to choose his cross, but leaves God to choose for him. He is content with both for the kind and the duration. A contented spirit says, "Let God apply what medicine He pleases, and let it remain as long as it will, I know that, when it has done its cure and eaten the venom of sin out of my heart, God will take it off again."

In a word, a contented Christian, being sweetly captivated under the authority of the Word, desires to be wholly at God's disposal, and is willing to live in that sphere and climate where God has set him. And if at any time he has been an instrument of doing noble and brave service in public, he knows he is but a rational tool, a servant to authority, and is content to return to his former private condition of life.

Cincinnatus, after he had done worthily and purchased for himself great fame in his dictatorship, notwith-

standing afterwards voluntarily returned to till and ma-
nure his four acres of ground. Thus should it be with
Christians, professing godliness with contentment lest
they display to the world only a brutish valor, being so un-
tamed and headstrong that when they have conquered
others yet they are not able to rule their own spirits.

5. He who is contented with his condition will not run
into sin to rid himself of trouble. I do not deny that a
Christian may lawfully seek to change his condition (so far
as God's providence guides him, he may follow); but some
men will not follow Providence, but run before it. As one
said, "This evil is of the Lord; why should I wait any
longer?" (2 Kings 6:33). If God does not open the door by
His providence, they will break it open and wind themselves out of affliction by sin, bringing their souls into
trouble by bringing their estates out of trouble. This is far
from holy contentment; this is unbelief breaking out into
rebellion.

A contented Christian is willing to wait for God's
leisure, and will not stir until God opens a door. As Paul
said in another case, "They have beaten us openly uncon-
demned, being Romans, and have cast us into prison; and
now do they thrust us out privily? Nay, verily; but let them
come themselves and fetch us out" (Acts 16:37). So with
reverence, says the contented Christian, "God has cast me
into this condition; and though it is sad and troublesome,
yet I will not stir till God, by a clear providence, fetches
me out."

Thus those brave-spirited Christians in Hebrews 11:35
did not accept deliverance upon base, dishonorable
terms. They would rather stay in prison than purchase
their liberty by carnal compliance. Estius observes that
they might not only have had their freedom, but been

raised to honor and put into offices of trust; yet the honor of religion was dearer to them than either liberty or worldly honor.

A contented Christian will not move till, like the Israelites, he sees a pillar of cloud and fire going before him. "It is good that a man should both hope and quietly wait for the salvation of the Lord" (Lamentations 3:26). It is good to await God's leisure, and not to extricate ourselves out of trouble until we see the star of God's providence pointing out a way to us.

Chapter 14

Rules about Contentment

I now proceed to a use of direction, to show Christians how they may attain to this divine art of contentment. Certainly it is feasible; others of God's saints have reached it. Paul, in our text, had it; and what do we think of those we read of in that little book of martyrs in Hebrews 11 who had trials of cruel mockings and scourgings, who wandered about in deserts and caves, yet were content? So it is possible to have contentment, and here I shall lay down some rules for attaining holy contentment.

Rule 1. Advance Faith

All our disquiets issue immediately from unbelief. It is this that raises the storm of discontent in the heart. Oh, set faith to work! It is the property of faith to silence our doubts, to scatter our fears, to still the heart when the passions are up. Faith works the heart to a sweet, serene composure. It is not having food and raiment, but having faith which will make us content. Faith chides down passion. When reason begins to sink, let faith swim.

QUESTION. How does faith work contentment?

ANSWER. Faith shows the soul that whatever its trials are, yet it is from the hand of a Father. It is indeed a bitter cup, but "shall I not drink the cup which My Father hath given Me to drink?" It is in love for my soul, faith shows me, that God corrects with the same love with which He crowns me. God is now training me for heaven. He carves

me to make me a polished shaft. These sufferings bring
forth patience, humility, even "the peaceable fruit of righteousness" (Hebrews 12:11); and if God can bring such
sweet fruit out of a sour stock, let Him graft me where He
pleases. Thus faith brings the heart to holy contentment.
    Faith sucks the honey of contentment out of the hive
of the promise. Christ is the vine; the promises are the
clusters of grapes that grow upon this vine; and faith
presses the sweet vine of contentment out of these spiritual clusters of the promises. I will show you but one clus-
ter: "The Lord will give grace and glory" (Psalm 84:11).
Here is enough faith to live upon. The promise is the
flower out of which faith distills the spirits and
quintessence of divine contentment. In a word, faith carries the soul up and makes it aspire after more noble and
generous delights than earth affords, and to live in the
world above the world. Would you lead contented lives?
Live up to the height of your faith.

Rule 2. Labor for Assurance
    Oh, let us get the interest cleared between God and
our own souls! Interest is a pleasing word much in use—
interest in great friends, earning interest on money. Oh, if
there is an interest worth looking after, it is an interest between God and the soul! Labor to say, "My God." To be
without money, without friends, and without God, too, is
sad. But he whose faith flourishes into assurance, who can
say, like Paul, "I know in whom I have believed" (2 Timothy 1:12), that man has enough to give his heart contentment. When a man's debts are paid and he can go abroad
without fear of being arrested, what contentment is this!
Oh, let your title be cleared! If God is ours, whatever we
lack in the creature is definitely made up in Him.

Do I lack bread? I have Christ, the Bread of Life. Am I under defilement? His blood is like the trees of the sanctuary: not only for meat, but for medicine. If anything in the world is worth laboring for, it is to get sound evidences that God is ours. Once this is cleared, what can come amiss? No matter what storms I meet with, I know where to put in for harbor. He who has God to be his God is so well contented with His condition that he does not much care whether he has anything else. To rest in a condition where a Christian cannot say God is his God is a matter of fear, and, if he can say so truthfully and is not content, it is a matter of shame. David encouraged himself in the Lord his God. It was sad with him: Ziklag had been burned, his wives had been taken captive, he had lost all, and he would likely have lost his soldiers' hearts too (for they spoke of stoning him), yet he had the ground of contentment within him—an interest in God—and this was a pillar of support to his spirit. He who knows God is his, and that all that is in God is for his good—if this does not satisfy him, nothing will.

Rule 3. Get a Humble Spirit

The humble man is the contented man. If his state is low, his heart is lower than his state. Therefore, be content. If his esteem in the world is low, he who is little in his own eyes will not be troubled much to be little in the eyes of others. He has a meaner opinion of himself than others can have of him. The humble man studies his own unworthiness. He looks upon himself as less than the least of God's mercies, and then a little will content him. He cries out with Paul that he is "the chief of sinners," and therefore does not murmur, but admire. He does not say that his comforts are small, but that his sins are great. He thinks it is a mercy that he is out of hell; therefore he is contented. He does not go to carve out a happier condition for himself; he knows the worst piece God cuts him is better than he deserves.

A proud man is never content; he is one who has a high opinion of himself. Therefore under small blessings he is disdainful; under small crosses he is impatient. The humble spirit is the contented spirit. If his cross is light, he reckons it in the inventory of his mercies. If it is heavy, yet he takes it upon his knees, knowing that when his state is worse it is to make him better. Where you lay humility for the foundation, contentment will be the superstructure.

Rule 4. Keep a Clear Conscience

Contentment is the manna that is laid up in the ark of a good conscience. Oh, take heed of indulging any sin! It is as natural for guilt to breed disquiet as for putrid matter to breed vermin. Sin lies as Jonah in the ship: it raises a tempest. If dust or particles get into the eye, they make the eye water and cause a soreness in it. If the eye is clear, then it is free from that soreness. If sin gets into the conscience, which is the eye of the soul, then grief and disquiet breed there. But keep the eye of conscience clear and all is well. What Solomon said of a good stomach, I may say of a good conscience: "To the hungry soul every bitter thing is sweet" (Proverbs 27:7). And so to a good conscience every bitter thing is sweet. It can pick contentment out of the cross.

Good conscience turns the waters of Marah into wine. Would you have a quiet heart? Get a smiling conscience. I do not wonder when I hear Paul say he was content in every state, when he could make that triumphant statement,

"I have lived in all good conscience to this day" (Acts 23:1). When a man's reckonings are clear, it must let in an abundance of contentment into the heart. Good conscience can suck contentment out of the bitterest drug. Under slanders, "This is our rejoicing, the testimony of our conscience" (2 Corinthians 1:12). In case of imprisonment, Paul had his prison songs, and could play the sweet lesson of contentment when his feet were in the stocks. Augustine has called it "the paradise of a good conscience"; and if it is so, then in prison we may be in paradise.

When the times are troublesome, good conscience makes it calm. If the conscience is clear, so what if the days are cloudy? Is it not a contentment to have a friend always by to speak a good word for us? Such a friend is conscience. Good conscience, as David's harp, drives away the evil spirit of discontent. When thoughts begin to arise and the heart is disquieted, conscience says to a man, as the king did to Nehemiah, "Why is thy countenance sad?" (Nehemiah 2:2). So says conscience, "Have you not the seed of God in you? Are you not an heir of the promise? Have you not a treasure that you can never be plundered of? Why is your countenance sad?" Oh, keep your conscience clear and you shall never want contentment! For a man to keep the pipes of his body, the veins and arteries, free from colds and obstructions is the best way to maintain health. In the same way, to keep conscience clear and preserve it from the obstructions of guilt is the best way to maintain contentment. First conscience is pure, and then peaceable.

Rule 5. Learn to Deny Yourselves
Look well to your affections; bridle them in. Do two

things: mortify your desires and moderate your delights.

1. Mortify your desires. We must not be of the dragon's temper who, they say, is so thirsty that no water will quench his thirst. "Mortify therefore your inordinate affections" (Colossians 3:5). In the Greek it is "your evil affection," to show that our desires, when they are inordinate, are evil. Crucify your desires. Be as dead men; a dead man has no appetite.

QUESTION. How should a Christian martyr his desires?

ANSWER. Get a right judgment of the things here below. They are mean, beggarly things. "Wilt thou set thine eyes upon that which is not?" (Proverbs 23:5) The appetite must be guided by reason. The affections are the feet of the soul; therefore they must follow the judgment, not lead it.

Seriously meditate often on mortality. Death will soon crop those flowers which we delight in, and pull down the fabric of those bodies which we so garnish and beautify. Think, when you are locking up your money in your chest, that someone shall shortly lock you up in your coffin.

2. Moderate your delights. Set not your hearts too much upon any creature. What we over-love, we shall over-grieve. Rachel set her heart too much upon her children, and when she had lost them she lost herself, too. Such a vein of grief was opened as could not be stanched; she refused to be comforted. Here was discontent. When we let any creature lie too near our heart, if God pulls away that comfort a piece of our heart is rent away with it. Too much fondness ends in frowardness. Those who would be content in the want of mercies must be moderate in the enjoyment of them. Jonathan dipped the rod in honey; he did not thrust it in. Let us take heed of engulfing our-

selves in pleasure. It is better to have a spare diet than, by
having too much, to satiate ourselves.

Rule 6. Get Much of Heaven into Your Heart
Spiritual things satisfy. The more of heaven that is in
us, the less earth will content. When a person has once
tasted the love of God, his thirst is much quenched toward
earthly things. The joys of God's Spirit are heart-filling
and heart-cheering joys. He who has these has heaven begun in him (Romans 14:17), and shall we not be content
to be in heaven? Oh, get a sublime heart! "Seek the things
that are above" (Colossians 3:1). Fly aloft in your affections; thirst after the graces and comforts of the Spirit.
The eagle that flies above in the air does not fear the
stinging of the serpent. The serpent creeps on his belly
and stings only those creatures that go upon the earth.
Discontent is a serpent that stings only an earthly
heart. A heavenly soul that, with the eagle, flies aloft finds
abundantly enough in God to give contentment, and is
not stung with the cares and disquiets of the world.

*Rule 7. Look Not So Much on the Dark Side of Your Condition as
on the Light Side*
God checkers His providences black and white, as the
pillar of cloud had its light and dark side. Look on the
light side of your state. Who looks on the back side of a
landscape? Suppose that you are in a lawsuit; there is the
dark side. Yet you have some land left; there is the light
side. You have sickness in your body; there is the dark
side. But you have grace in your soul; there is the light
side. You have a child taken away; there is the dark side.
Your husband lives; there is the light side. God's providences in this life are various, represented by those speck-

that from within which is able to support him. He has that strength of faith and good hope through grace as will bear up his heart in the deficiency of outward comforts. The philosophers of old, when their estates were gone, yet could take contentment in the goods of the mind, their learning and virtue; and shall not a believer find much more in the grace of the Spirit, that rich enamel and embroidery of the soul? Say to yourself, "If friends leave me, if riches take wings, yet I have that within that comforts me, a heavenly treasure. When the blossoms of my estate are blown off, still there is the sap of contentment in the root of my heart. I still have an interest in God, and that interest cannot be broken off." Oh, never place your felicity in these dull and beggarly things here below!

Rule 10. Let Us Often Compare Our Condition.
QUESTION. How should I compare?
ANSWER. Make this fivefold comparison:
1. Let us compare our condition with what we deserve. If we do not have what we desire, we have more than we deserve. As for our mercies, we have deserved less; as for our afflictions, we have deserved more.

First, in regard to our mercies, we have deserved less. What can we deserve? Can man be profitable to the Almighty? We live upon free grace. Alexander gave a great gift to one of his subjects. The man, being quite taken with it, said, "This is more than I am worthy of." The king said, "I do not give you this because you are worthy of it, but I give a gift worthy of Alexander." Whatever we have is not merit, but bounty. The least bit of bread is more than God owes us. We can bring faggots to our own burning, but not one flower to the garland of our salvation. He who has the least mercy will die in God's debt.

Second, in regard to our afflictions, we have deserved more. "Thou hast punished us less than our iniquities deserve" (Ezra 9:13). Is our condition sad? We deserve a worse one. Has God taken away our estate from us? He might have taken away Christ from us. Has He thrown us into prison? He might have thrown us into hell. He might as well damn us as whip us. This should make us content.

2. Let us compare our condition with others, and this will make us content. We look at those who are above us; let us look at those who are below us. We see one in his silks, another in his sackcloth. One has the waters of a full cup wrung out to him; another is mingling his drink with tears. How many pale faces do we behold whom not sickness, but want has brought into a consumption? Think of this and be content. It is worse with them who, perhaps, deserve better than we, and are higher in God's favor. Am I in prison? Was not Daniel in a worse place, the lions' den?

Do I live in a mean cottage? Look on those who are banished from their houses. We read that the primitive saints "wandered up and down in sheepskins and goatskins, of whom the world was not worthy" (Hebrews 11:37–38). Do you have a gentle fit of a fever or shivering? Look on those who are tormented with the stone and gout.

Others of God's children have had greater afflictions, and have borne them better than we. Daniel fed upon vegetables and drank water, yet was fairer than those who ate of the king's portion. Some Christians who have been in a lower condition, who have fed upon vegetables and water, have looked better, and have been more patient and content than we who enjoy abundance. Do others rejoice in affliction, and do we repine? Can they take up their cross and walk cheerfully under it, and do we, under a lighter cross, murmur?

3. Let us compare our condition with Christ's upon earth. What a poor, mean condition was He pleased to be in for us! He was content with anything. "For ye know the grace of our Lord Jesus Christ, that though He was rich, yet for your sakes He became poor" (2 Corinthians 8:9). He could have brought down a house from heaven with Him, or challenged the high places of earth; but He was content to be in the wine press that we might be in the wine cellar, and to live poor that we might die rich. The manger was His cradle, the cobwebs His canopy. He who is now preparing mansions for us in heaven had none for Himself on earth. He had nowhere to lay His head. Christ came in the form of a pauper, "Who being in the form of God took upon Him the form of a servant" (Philippians 2:6–7). We do not read of any sums of money that He had. When He wanted money, He was forced to work a miracle for it (Matthew 17:27). Jesus Christ was in a low condition. He was never high, except when He was lifted up upon the cross, and that was His humility. He was content to live poor and die cursed. Oh, compare your condition with Christ's!

4. Let us compare our condition with what it was once, and this will make us content.

First, let us compare our spiritual state with what it once was. What were we when we lay in our blood? We were heirs apparent to hell, having no right to pluck one leaf from the tree of the promise. It was a Christless and hopeless condition (Ephesians 2:12), but now God has cut off the entail of hell and damnation. He has taken you out of the wild olive of nature and engrafted you into Christ, making you living branches of that living Vine. He has not only caused the light to shine upon you, but into you (2 Corinthians 4:6), and has given you a legal right to all the privileges of sonship. Is not here that which may make the soul content?

Second, let us compare our temporal state with what it once was. Alas, we had nothing when we stepped out of the womb, "for we brought nothing with us into the world" (1 Timothy 6:7). If we do not have what we desire, we have more than we brought with us. We brought nothing but sin. Other creatures bring something with them into the world. The lamb brings wool and the silkworm brings silk, but we brought nothing with us. What if our condition is low at present? It is better than it once was. Therefore, "having food and raiment, let us be content" (1 Timothy 6:8). Whatever we have, God's providence fetched it in to us; and if we lose all, yet we have as much as we brought with us. This was what made Job content: "Naked came I out of my mother's womb" (Job 1:21). It is as if he had said, "Though God has taken all away from me, yet why should I murmur? I am as rich now as I was when I came into the world. I have as much left as I brought with me. Naked came I hither. Therefore, blessed be the name of the Lord."

5. Let us compare our condition with what it shall be shortly. There is a time coming shortly when, if we had all the riches of India, they would do us no good. We must die and can carry nothing with us. So the apostle says, "It is certain we can carry nothing out of the world" (1 Timothy 6:7); therefore it follows, "having food and raiment, let us be content" (verse 8). Open the rich man's grave and see what is there. You may find the miser's bones, but not his riches. Were we to live forever here, or could we carry our riches into another world, then indeed we might

be discontented when we look upon our empty bags; but it is not so. God may presently seal a death warrant to apprehend us, and when we die, we cannot carry our estate with us. Honor and riches do not descend into the grave. Why, then, are we troubled at our outward condition? Why do we disguise ourselves with discontent? Oh, lay up a stock of grace! Be rich in faith and good works, for these riches follow us (Revelation 14:13). No other coin but grace will be accepted as currency in heaven. Silver and gold will not go there. Labor to be rich towards God (Luke 12:21). As for other things, do not be solicitous; we shall carry nothing with us.

Rule 11. Do Not Bring Your Condition to Your Mind, but Bring Your Mind to Your Conditon
The way for a Christian to be content is not by raising his state higher, but by bringing his spirit lower; not by making his barns wider, but his heart narrower. One man will not be contented with a whole lordship or manor; another is satisfied with a few acres of land. What is the difference? The one studies to satisfy curiosity, the other necessity; the one thinks of what he may have, the other of what he may spare.

Rule 12. Study the Vanity of the Creature
It does not matter whether we have more or less of these things; they have vanity written upon the frontispiece of them. The world is like a shadow that declines. It is delightful, but deceitful; it promises more than we find, and it fails us when we have the most need of it. All the world rings changes and is constant only in its disappointments. What, then, if we have less of that which is, at best, voluble and fluid? The world is as full of mutation as

motion, and what if God cuts us short in worldly things?
The more a man has to do with the world, the more he
has to do with vanity. The world may be compared to ice,
which is smooth but slippery, or to the Egyptian temples,
which are very beautiful and sumptuous on the outside,
but within which there is nothing to be seen but the image of an ape. Every creature says about satisfaction, "It is
not in me."

The world is not a filling but a fleeting comfort. It is
like a game of tennis. Providence bandies her golden balls
first to one, then to another. Why are we discontented at
the loss of these things? Only because we expect that from
them which is not, and depend on them for that which we
ought not. "Jonah was exceeding glad of the gourd"
(Jonah 4:6). What vanity was it? Is it much to see a withering gourd smitten, or to see the moon dressing itself in a
new shape and figure?

Rule 13. Get Fancy Regulated

It is the fancy which raises the price of things above
their real worth. What is the reason why one tulip is worth
five pounds and another perhaps is not worth one
shilling? Fancy raises the price. The difference is rather
imaginary than real. Why should it be better to have thousands than hundreds? Because men fancy it so. If we could
fancy a lower condition as better, as having less care in it
and less account, it would be far more desirable. The water that springs out of the rock tastes as sweet as if it came
out of a golden chalice. Things are as we fancy them.

Ever since the Fall the fancy is distempered. "God saw
that the imagination of the thoughts of his heart was evil"
(Genesis 6:5). Fancy looks through wrong spectacles. Pray
that God will sanctify your fancy. A lower condition would

content you if the mind and fancy were set right. Diogenes preferred his cynical life before Alexander's royalty. He fancied his little cloister best. Fabricius was a poor man, yet despised the gold of King Pyrrhus.

> Fabricus, content with his little honorable portion,
>   used to despise the gifts of kings,
> And the Roman consul Serranus used to toil with
>   the heavy plow.
>
> (Claudius)

Could we cure a distempered fancy, we might soon conquer a discontented heart.

Rule 14. Consider How Little Will Suffice

The body is only of small capacity, and is easily restored. Christ has taught us to pray for our daily bread. Nature is contented with a little.

"Not to thirst and not to starve is enough," said Gregory Nazianzus. "Meat and drink is a Christian's riches," said St. Jerome; and the apostle said, "Having food and raiment, let us be content."

> O luxuriance, wasteful of things, never contented
>   with its little provision,
> And hunger, ambitious for food sought out on sea
>   and land, and for the glory of a sumptuous table!
> Teach us with how little it is permitted to lead forth
>   our life, and how much nature seeks after.
>
> (Lucan, *Pharsalia* 1.4)

The stomach is sooner filled than the eye. How quickly would a man be content if he would study to satisfy his hunger rather than his humor?

Rule 15. Believe that the Present Condition is Best for Us

Flesh and blood is not a competent judge. Satiated stomachs prefer banqueting stuff, but a man who regards his health would rather have solid food. Vain men fancy such a condition to be best, and would flourish in their bravado; whereas a wise Christian has his will melted into God's will and thinks it best to have whatever God directs. God is wise. He knows whether we need food or medicine; and if we could acquiesce with Providence, the quarrel would soon be at an end. Oh, what a strange creature would man be if he were what he could wish himself to be! Be content to be at God's allowance. God knows which is the fittest pasture to put His sheep in. Sometimes a barren ground does well, whereas a fine pasture may rot.

Do I meet with such a cross? God shows me what the world is. He has no better way to wean me than by putting me with a stepmother. Does God stop my allowance? He is now dieting me. Do I meet with losses? It is that God may keep me from being lost. Every crosswind shall at last blow me to the right port. If we believed that condition to be best which God parcels out to us, we would cheerfully submit and say, "The lines are fallen in pleasant places."

Rule 16. Do Not Indulge the Flesh Too Much

We have taken an oath in baptism to forsake the flesh. The flesh is a worse enemy than the devil; it is a bosom traitor. An enemy within is worst. If there were no devil to tempt, the flesh would be another Eve to tempt us to the forbidden fruit. Oh, take heed of giving way to it! Where does all our discontent come from but the fleshly part? The flesh puts us upon the immoderate pursuit of the world. It seeks after ease and plenty, and, if it is not satisfied, then discontents begin to arise. Oh, let it not have the reins; martyr the flesh. In spiritual things, the flesh is a sluggard; in secular things it is a horseleech crying, "Give, give." The flesh is an enemy to suffering; it will sooner make a man a courtier than a martyr. Oh, keep it under; put its neck under Christ's yoke; stretch and nail it to His cross! Never let a Christian look for contentment in his spirit until there is confinement in his flesh.

Rule 17. Meditate Much on the Glory Which Shall Be Revealed
There are great things laid up in heaven. Though it is sad for the present, yet let us be content in that it will shortly be better. It is but awhile and we shall be with Christ, bathing our souls in the fountain of His love. We shall never complain of wants or injuries any more. Our cross may be heavy, but one sight of Christ will make us forget all our former sorrows. There are two things that should give contentment:
1. God will make us able to bear our troubles (1 Corinthians 10:13). God, said Chrysostom, is like one who plays the lute. He will not let the strings of his lute be too slack lest it spoil the music; nor will he suffer them to be stretched too hard or screwed too lightly lest they break. So does God deal with us. He will not let us have too much prosperity, lest this spoil the music of prayer and repentance; nor will He let us have too much adversity, lest the "spirit fail before me, and the souls which He has made" (Isaiah 57:16).
2. When we have suffered awhile, we shall be perfected in glory. The cross shall be our ladder by which we shall climb up to heaven. Be then content, and the scene will alter. God will, before long, turn our water into wine. The hope of this is enough to drive away all distempers from the heart. Blessed be God, it will be better. "We have no

continuing city here" (Hebrews 13:14). Therefore, our affections cannot continue. A wise man still looks to the end. "The end of a just man is peace" (Psalm 37:37). I think the smoothness of the end should make amends for the ruggedness of the way.

Oh, eternity, eternity! Think often of the kingdom prepared. David was advanced from the field to the throne. First he held his shepherd's staff, and shortly after that the royal scepter. God's people may be put to hard services here, but God has chosen them to be kings to sit upon the throne with the Lord Jesus. This, being weighed in the balance of faith, would be an excellent means to bring the heart to contentment.

Rule 18. Be Much in Prayer

The last rule for contentment is to be much in prayer. Beg God that He will work our hearts into this blessed frame. "Is any man afflicted? Let him pray" (James 5:13). Similarly, is any man discontented? Let him pray. Prayer gives vent. The opening of a vein lets out bad blood. When the heart is filled with sorrow and disquiet, prayer lets out the bad blood. The key of prayer, oiled with tears, unlocks the heart of all its discontents. Prayer is a holy spell or charm to drive away trouble. Prayer is the unbosoming of the soul, the unloading of all our cares into God's breast; and this ushers in sweet contentment.

When there is any burden upon our spirits, by opening our mind to a friend we find our hearts pleasantly eased and quieted. It is not our strong resolutions, but our strong requests to God which must give the heart ease in trouble. By prayer, the strength of Christ is brought into the soul, and where that is a man is able to go through any condition. Paul could be content in every state, but you

ought not to think that he was able to do that of himself.
He tells you that though he could want and abound and
do all things, yet it was through Christ strengthening him
(Philippians 4:13). It is the child who writes, but it is the
scribe who guides his hand. Paul arrived at the hardest
duty in religion, contentment, but the Spirit was his pilot
and Christ his strength; and this strength was ushered in
by holy prayer. Prayer is a powerful orator. Prayer is an
exorcist with God and an exorcist against sin. The best way
is to pray down discontent. What Luther said of concupis-
cence, I may say of discontent: prayer is a sacred leech to
suck out the venom and swelling of this passion. Prayer
composes the heart and brings it into tune. Has God de-
prived you of many comforts? Bless God that He left you
the spirit of prayer.

Chapter 15

Use of Comfort

The last use is of comfort, or an encouraging word to the contented Christian. If there is a heaven upon earth, you have it. Oh, Christian, you may leap over your troubles and, with the Leviathan, laugh at the shaking of a spear (Job 41:29)! What shall I say? You are a crown to your profession; you hold out to all the world that there's virtue enough in religion to give the soul contentment. You show the height of grace. When grace is crowning, it is not so much for us to be content, but when grace is conflicting, and meets with crosses, temptations, and agonies, now to be content is a glorious thing indeed.

To a contented Christian I shall say two things for a farewell:

First, God is exceedingly taken with such a frame of heart. God said of a contented Christian, as David said of Goliath's sword, "There is none like that; give it me" (1 Samuel 21:9). If you would please God and be men of His heart, be content. It is said that Rebecca made Isaac savory meat such as her husband loved. Would you give God such a dish as He loves? Bring Him this dish of contentment. The musician has many lessons to play, but he has one above all the rest. There are many lessons of holy music that delight God—the lessons of repentance, humility, and the like—but this lesson of contentment is the sweetest lesson that a believer can play. God hates a froward spirit.

Second, the contented Christian shall be no loser. What did Job lose by his patience? God gave him three times as much as he had before. What did Abram lose by his contentment? He was content to leave his country at God's call; the Lord made a covenant with him that he would be His God (Genesis 17). He changed his name so that it was no longer Abram, but Abraham, the father of many nations. God made his seed as the stars of heaven and honored him with this title: "the father of the faithful." The Lord made known his secrets to him. "Shall I hide from Abraham the thing I will do?" (Genesis 18:17). God settled a rich inheritance upon him, the land which was a type of heaven, and afterwards translated him into the blessed paradise.

God will be sure to reward the contented Christian. As our Savior said in another case to Nathanael, "Because I said I saw thee under the fig tree, believest thou? Thou shalt see greater things than these" (John 1:50), so I say: are you content with a little, O Christian? You shall see greater things than these. God will distill the sweet influences of His love into your soul. He will raise friends up for you. He will bless the oil in the jar and, when that is done, He will crown you with an eternal enjoyment of Himself. He will give you heaven where you shall have as much contentment as your soul can possibly thirst after.